UK Branch of the International
Association of Former Officials
of the European Union (AIACE)

Changing
Horizons

Memories of Britain's European Pioneers 1973

Edited by Martin Vasey
with Robert Elphick and Robert Hull

Contents

The pressmen

Epilogue

Appendices

Foreword

Richard Hay

Dear Reader

Forty years is a long time. Over those years we in the United Kingdom have seen what we then called the Common Market change and develop from a European Community of nine member states to a European Union of 28. In the UK this enterprise has rarely been out of political debate. Whatever one now thinks about the UK's membership, accession in 1973 was certainly a significant step in this country's history. Its 40th anniversary should not go unnoticed.

The present publication recognises this special milestone, by gathering together the memories of people who then went to work in one of the European institutions.

It is not meant as a contribution to current disputes about UK membership of the EU. Recollections of 40 years ago are a poor guide to the present. The whole enterprise has evolved a great deal. And the way the institutions work has also changed. Those who know the European institutions now may not recognise many of the names then used to describe the way the organisations worked (we provide a short glossary). Relative salaries of EU staff have fallen, their work pressure has increased, total staff numbers have risen through successive enlargements from some 15,000 to 55,000 (though still, for all 28 countries, only to the level of the staff employed by one major city in the UK).

Rather, these pieces try to capture what experience of accession meant at the time to a few of those who changed careers (and usually home and country, too) to turn UK membership into reality. For many, it felt like being a pioneer. We have gathered short contributions from some of those who went to work for the European Community in 1973 or thereabouts, whether as senior policy official, secretary, lawyer, linguist, scientist or nurse. We asked them to write of their experiences and their feelings at the time. Nearly all are members of the UK Branch of the International Association of Former Officials of the European Union; a few are guests. To help set the scene, we have also included a large part of a lecture given in 1999 by the late Lord Thomson, one of the UK's first European Commissioners, because he describes very well the experiences and the challenges of 1973. And as an epilogue to give a wider picture, we also include a brief summary of the results of a study of this early UK recruitment, drawn from an academic study.

We hope that their memories of their part in the process of UK accession, in a world that was in many ways very different from the present, will awaken memories of that time among our readers. We hope, too, that this venture into the past will deepen understanding of the present. These words are written by those who then performed an act, in Shakespeare's words, "whereof what's past is prologue; what's to come, in yours and my discharge."

This collection has not come together without a great deal of work. First, of course, we are very grateful to those who have been ready to write for this publication. Their work has been edited by Martin Vasey, helped by Robert Elphick, Robert Hull and latterly Tony Robinson; putting together texts from so many authors has not been easy, or light, and we acknowledge hard work and skill. We also thank those who hold copyright for the few passages for which their permission had to be sought.

The production has been done, skilfully and willingly, by the staff of the Office for Infrastructure and Logistics, Brussels, a service of the European Commission; they have done this as part of the limited support which the EU institutions give to the different parts of our Association which now brings together 9,500 former officials with branches in 15 countries. We wish to thank them, and in particular their Director Eric Halskov, the designer Stefano Mattei, and the whole production team.

On behalf of the UK Branch, and of you, as a reader, I warmly thank each person who has made this publication possible. We very much hope you will enjoy it.

Richard Hay
Chair, UK Branch
International Association of Former Employees of the European Union
July 2013

The BBC's man in Brussels

Robert Elphick

When did the UK actually join Europe?

You can have plenty of arguments over the real moment when the United Kingdom became a full part of the European Community. Perhaps only I know the secret of how and when exactly the knot was tied. I am prepared to let everyone in on it at the cost of a glass or two.

After all the rebuffs from the French and a wobbly persistence from British governments of both major parties, the Treaty of Rome was at last signed by the Prime Minister in the person of the Rt. Hon. Edward Heath on 22 January 1972.

I know that is true because I was in the Egmont Palace in Brussels when the deed was done. I remember how late Heath was for the ceremony and we all had to sit or in my case stand against the wall, trying to keep cool in the ornate but overheating chamber.

Since my task was to provide pictures and a story for BBC TV-News, I confess to feeling a bit miffed when it came out that the delay was caused by some woman. She had thrown a bottle of ink all over Ted Heath's nice city suit as he got out of his car outside the Palace. Fortunately one of my colleagues was on hand to get that, but the news filtered through only slowly into the chamber where all the usual dignitaries were gathered including the King of the Belgians. King Baudouin was a nice affable chap and I managed to have a word or two with him off the record, but I confess I forgot to ask him about the significance of the ink throwing.

Some people claim our fate was sealed on that occasion.

To my mind though, that was not the actual occasion for the cross-over for the UK from being a free-wheeling member of EFTA (the rival European Free Trade Area) to getting into bed with the rest of Europe as a member of the European Communities and later of course the European Union.

Was it then attendance at the special summit called by France's President, Georges Pompidou, for the newly enlarged EC? The Prime Ministers of the UK, Ireland and Denmark joined the original six in Paris in the autumn of 1972. It was quite a successful joining together; so pleased were they all that they signed a pledge to achieve full economic and political Union by 1980. I managed to collar Ted Heath at Le Bourget airport on departure to ask him what it meant. He confessed he didn't know either. It was a pledge though that very quietly was left to drift to oblivion.

But no, I wouldn't say that that date was definitive either.

What about 5 January, 1973, when our new Commissioners arrived in Brussels to take up their tasks?

It was a day of dreadful weather. Fog clung to the entire northern part of Europe and the continent was well and truly isolated. This meant that Sir Christopher Soames and George Thomson couldn't get into the airport at Zaventem and had to be diverted to an airport in Holland which by some miracle was briefly open.

The plan was then that they would then come down from the Netherlands by rail. We all had to wait for them on the down platform at Brussels' Gare du Nord station. With everything clinging wet, it was a miserable gathering; a few journalists and the newly appointed *chefs de cabinet* of our new Commissioners. David Hannay, waiting for Soames, was looking a mite worried. "Oh God, the old man will be in a frightful mood," I remember him saying.

But it wasn't as bad as that. The UK's champions seemed resigned to their new role. They uttered a few words for us to report, none of which I can recall now. And we went our several ways to sit it out in the Berlaymont while the Commission President, Xavier Ortoli, spent the night with his colleagues to share out portfolios. That went well and they held the first Commission meeting of the new regime in a reasonably good humour, Soames with responsibility for External Affairs and Thomson looking after the new Regional Policy dossier.

But I believe that for the general public the real watershed in our island story can be detected a few days earlier.

As the final minutes of 1972 ticked away, most of the British contingent in Brussels were well into a good old knees-up party at the Queen Vic. This was a rather up-market pub on the Rond Point Schuman just across from the Commission's old Berlaymont headquarters but which unhappily fell victim to the vicious competition for beer drinkers that the capital of Europe offers. There was a lot of noise and singing of patriotic songs. I remember we celebrated the 1973 New Year and the UK's newer status in Europe twice: once as the local clocks chimed midnight and an hour later when Big Ben did the same.

But even then, I was not quite satisfied that the line had finally been drawn.

My task, simply put, was to give pictures to the BBC and through them to the great British public and then the wider world to prove that all was changed forever.

On New Year's day, I conceived the idea then of showing British civil servants streaming into the Berlaymont Building to take up the burden of running Europe alongside their new Continental colleagues.

The problem was that it was a public holiday and the doors were locked and barred. There was no streaming except from the heavens. Fortunately in my earlier months of poking about in Brussels, I had made the acquaintance of the janitors, the canny people who ran the building. They had been most helpful in getting me into forbidden places before, and I found salvation with them again.

One of them was doing duty in his den despite the holiday. He listened to my plea for help and rustled around behind his desk where he kept the flags of all nations.

While we set the camera up outside, he expertly ran the Union Jack up the tallest flagpole in front of the building.

The pictures appeared on the evening news bulletins pretty well everywhere.

That's when I reckon people really knew there was no going back.

One of the first
UK Commissioners

George Thomson

Journey to an Unknown Destination[1]

Christopher Soames and I … had been much involved in Britain's relations within the European Community. I had been in the Cabinet as Minister for Europe, preparing the approach to our negotiations for entry, and Christopher had been a Labour Government appointment as Ambassador in Paris. We were to discover, however, that although we knew a good deal about the European Commission, a good deal of it was from the outside.

I approved the Cabinet paper with the draft of Britain's application to join in a hotel in my Dundee constituency just before Labour lost the General Election of May 1970. It was delivered by my Conservative successor, Tony Barber, almost word for word with only an opening preamble that the British Government had changed, but not the policy. It was a period of bi-partisanship between Government and Opposition, but it was not to last for long. By the time Soames and I went to Brussels, he had behind him a Prime Minister and a party which was by a great majority in favour of British entry. I came from the pro-Europe minority of a divided Opposition. The European issue had reasserted its deeply divisive impact on British politics.

Christopher Soames and I came from very different backgrounds - political and otherwise - but Christopher proved a good man to go tiger hunting with in the jungles of the Berlaymont. Not for nothing, when Christopher Soames was leaving as Ambassador in Paris, did his favourite restaurateur remark *"une grande ambience est partie"*. Christopher felt that nothing less than a plane of the Queen's Flight would do for our historic arrival in Brussels. Unfortunately that morning there was a Royal pre-emption of the plane on which we planned to travel, and we were left with the more modest end of the Queen's Flight which turned out to be the Board of Trade calibration plane. No glasses of champagne; only instant coffee in plastic cups in the midst of a flying laboratory! And the weather was foul. So in the most literal sense we found ourselves making a journey to an unknown destination. We had to be diverted to a local Dutch airfield. When we arrived, trudging across the tarmac with our briefcases, we found the terminal locked for lunch. If only The Daily Express had got a photograph at that moment of two portly Commissioners visibly sagging before that locked door! So this is Europe!

1   Extracts from a lecture delivered at the Foreign and Commonwealth Office on 27 October, 1999, by Lord Thomson of Monifieth, published as FCO Historians Occasional Paper No 16, and reprinted with permission.

However, the Europe of Brussels proved very welcoming when we finally reached it that night. Given the chequered relations between Britain and the Community (subsequently), it is worth recalling the extraordinary enthusiasm there was in 1973 for the entry of Britain and of Ireland and Denmark. After years of indecision by Britain and after two vetoes by President de Gaulle, this first enlargement from the original six was regarded as a major milestone. Out of the whole quarter century to follow, 1973 has turned out to be the only twelve months in which Britain was regarded by the rest of the Community as fully participating with her partners in the next stage of the Community's voyage. The fact that the Labour Party had swung from seeking membership in 1970 to opposing it in 1972 on what they described as "Tory terms" was regarded as a passing problem of domestic politics, since most of the former Labour Ministers involved in preparing the negotiations with Europe had declared they found the terms acceptable. Such goodwill was invaluable in the early months as Britain set out on its learning curve about the internal workings of the Community institutions, and they, in their turn, found themselves adapting to some of the Anglo-Saxon (and Irish and Danish) political habits. A striking example of this two-way process occurred over time in the field of language. Despite elaborate interpretation arrangements, the working language of the policy papers was French. And the French were well known to be properly proud and protective of their national language. It was a considerable time before working papers arrived in English at the same time as in French. ...

The most immediate challenge, however, facing the UK in 1973 related to the British bid to fill posts in the Commission secretariat and in the other institutions. For the interested departments in Whitehall and for the two future Commissioners, it was an immensely difficult task, a multi-dimensional jig-saw puzzle. We could not know in advance which posts would be available for our bidding. The Byzantine nature of the appointments system with its dimension of political patronage was strange and alien to us.

There was a strong wish to ensure that the British contingent in Brussels was of high quality. We sought a mixture mainly of civil servants, but also people from business and industry and the universities with a sprinkling of political enthusiasts for the European ideal. We hoped that many would be attracted to stay and make their career as European civil servants, and that others, after useful experience in Brussels, would return with their career prospects at home enhanced by their knowledge of the workings of the Community... Twenty-five years on one cannot say that the British participation in the European civil service of the Commission has been as substantial as it ought to have been. At the higher levels in the Commission the UK produced from the beginning some very good directors and directors general, including of course Lord Williamson as the able successor as Secretary General to the legendary Emil Noel. With hindsight, however, I think the UK civil service failed to recognize the importance of posts in middle management, and of recruiting a big enough or good enough pool of younger Britons capable of working their way up the ladder.

For a British politician, there were many fascinating discoveries in those early days of entry of the differences between the Westminster and the continental political culture. For the first time I found myself working within a written constitution of the Treaty of Rome, A meeting of the Commission had a very superficial resemblance to the British Cabinet meeting with which I was familiar, but there at a side table sat the Service Juridique-the legal advisers to the Commission - who did not hesitate to intervene as custodians of the Treaty. How different from Downing Street where the Law officers appear rarely and only by special invitation. And yet ... and yet. Things are never quite what they seem in the European Union. I remember Sir Con O'Neill, that magnificent mandarin of the accession negotiations, telling me wryly that I would learn lessons in pragmatism in Brussels I had never dreamed of in the Fabian Society, He was right. I found the Commission (and equally the Council of Ministers where the final decisions were taken) tried with painstaking patience to reach agreements on its proposals by consensus after wide ranging consultations with outside interests sometimes lasting years. It was a more open, less secretive, institution than the Whitehall I had left…

As a British Cabinet Minister, I was expertly briefed only on matters of departmental interest. For the rest I was on my own, and not encouraged to trespass on the departmental territory of other Ministers. In Brussels I found myself equipped with a continental *cabinet* - a large Private Office with officials shadowing other areas of Commission policy. This enabled me to be well briefed on the CAP or other responsibilities of other Commissioners far removed from my own portfolio ... I have the confirmation of Lord Williamson that – and here I quote him – "… It is a complete misunderstanding to suggest, as some commentators do, that the *cabinets* simply battle to serve a national viewpoint. They were realistic about national concerns, but European in outlook."… When it was necessary to tell their colleagues what the national reaction to a proposal was likely to be - since no one else could perform that duty - a nice euphemism was used and we talked of "the country I know best".

In 1973 I found that the President of the Commission was much more "first amongst equals" than the myth attached to the position of British Prime Ministers. But the Commission Presidency suffered from some particular handicaps which have damaged the effectiveness of the Commission over the years. President Ortoli, an able Chairman with great previous experience of the Commission from the inside, had no influence over his choice of colleagues. Each of us emerged from the particular and sometimes peculiar political circumstances of the country from which we came. The President had some but not much influence over the distribution of portfolios. They emerged from discussions between the new Commissioners strongly influenced behind the scenes by the views of the member Governments. Once the posts were shared out the President had no powers during the four-year life of the Commission to bring about a re-shuffle. Still less could the President bring about the resignation of a Commissioner who failed to perform properly. There was only the ultimate deterrent of the Parliament proposing the removal of the entire Commission. …

From the beginning there has been a real problem for the Commission over its democratic legitimacy and its accountability. …

The European Parliament is steadily gaining a stronger constitutional role within the European Union. In 1973 it was no more than a consultative assembly. …

Until the first band of British MP's arrived in Strasbourg led by the redoubtable Sir Peter Kirk, a serious question-time hardly existed. For the Commission there was no time limit for the preparation of answers to questions. Ministers representing the Council had never heard of supplementary questions and were quite unaccustomed to the rough and tumble of a real Parliamentary question-time. They found it difficult to answer the simplest questions without making a speech full of Continental rhetoric. I recall one scene in which the Italian Foreign Minister, Signor [Amintore] Fanfani, collapsed almost in tears over the affront to his dignity in having to face a hostile Westminster-type cross examination. His own party supporters in Parliament felt obliged to present him with a large bouquet of flowers to console him! …

[One simple lesson to learn from those early days] is that membership of the Union does not involve abandoning the defence of British interests … I recall the remark of a wise Dutch Commissioner during the first years of British membership. "My dear George," he said, "there are now two countries in the Community who are stubborn about defending their national interests, France and Britain. But a word of advice," he added. "France always describes opposition to her position as a betrayal of Europe. Britain makes it appear as if Europe is betraying Britain. Not the best way to get results!" …

The underlying aim of the European construction from the beginning has been political not economic. Politicians in Britain have been accused of concealing this fact. I do not believe that the public declarations of those of us who took Britain into Europe in 1973 are open to that charge. …

The men from the FCO

David Hannay

Filling the top jobs in the Commission[2]

In the summer of 1973 Sir Christopher Soames offered me the job of *chef de cabinet*; and I signed on for four and a half years of gilded slavery which I enjoyed as much as anything I ever did in my professional life.

The title of *chef de cabinet* is not really translatable into English and no function like it existed or exists in Whitehall … Part of the job was identical to being the Principal Private Secretary of a British cabinet minister, … acting as a transmission belt between the Minister and the officials in his department. Another part of the job was acting as what would now be called a Political Adviser, a source of advice separate from and more politicised than that coming from the department. But a *chef de cabinet* in the Commission had an additional collective function which would certainly not have been found in any national capital. The *chefs de cabinet* of the Commissioners (at that time 13 of them) met together every Monday afternoon for several hours, under the chairmanship of the President's *chef de cabinet* and the tutelage of the Secretary-General of the Commission, Emile Noel, to prepare the Commission's own weekly meeting on Wednesday. The Commission agenda for each week was carefully sifted and reviewed, some items were discarded or delayed and major differences between Commissioners were identified. A good deal of negotiation was undertaken to remove minor differences and to clarify major ones. Woe betide a *chef de cabinet* who arrived at a meeting ill-prepared on any issue which his Commissioner was putting to the College. Noel, the avuncular but encyclopaedically knowledgeable French Socialist, who had been Secretary-General of the Commission since the Community was first established in 1957, would grill you rigorously, and, if ever he prefaced a sentence with *"Mais, cher ami … "*, you knew that you were in serious trouble. These collective meetings of *chefs de cabinet* were the basis on which Commissioners were briefed to enable them to intervene in policy areas for which they were not personally responsible - for example, agriculture or transport policy - the Commission being a much more collegiate body than any national cabinet. To handle this pretty considerable workload, each Commissioner had a staff allocation for his *cabinet* not too different from the Private Office of a major Whitehall ministry. At that time most, if not all, members of *cabinets,* apart from the President's *cabinet* which had always been multinational, tended to be of the same nationality as their Commissioner ….

2   Extract from David Hannay – *Britain's Quest for a Role, London* 2012, IB Tauris (ISBN 978 1 78076 056 8); reprinted with permission

From my appointment in the summer of 1972 until the summer of the next year my time was heavily absorbed in putting together the future Commissioner's personal staff (his *cabinet* in Commission parlance), in sifting the large number of British candidates for senior posts in the Community's institutions and then, once the new Commission had taken over at the beginning of 1973, in negotiating their placement in suitable jobs. Of these three tasks the first was the easiest and the last by far the most complex and difficult …

The challenge was to move fairly rapidly from a situation where there were literally no British nationals at policymaking level in any of the institutions (there were of course translators, interpreters and members of the Commission's London information office) to one where British nationals were occupying a share of posts at all levels which was roughly similar to that held by nationals of the three existing large member states, France, Germany and Italy.

Clearly this could not be done simply by the sort of entry grade competitive examinations which are the standing practice in modern bureaucracies, although such procedures were needed for the longer term future and were in fact put in hand as soon as we joined. But finding candidates at the director-general, deputy director-general, director and head of division level (a span roughly equivalent to Whitehall's grades between permanent secretary and principal) had to be done by careful scrutiny of CVs and by interview. In this process we were helped by the Civil Service Commission in London; and the Commissioners themselves interviewed all candidates for posts at the top two levels. While the prospect of a career in Brussels at a time when enthusiasm for Britain joining the Community was running high attracted many candidates of excellent quality, we had to be on our guard against a well-known tendency of senior management in such circumstances to unload people with whom they wished to dispense; and the Prime Minister's wise commitment to President Pompidou to ensure that British officials being sent to Brussels would have a reasonable working knowledge of French acted as another constraint. Anyway, we duly arrived in Brussels with a large portfolio of candidates but no very clear picture of precisely which jobs would be available for them to fill.

At the Commission end a kind of mirror-image exercise had been getting under way. It had been agreed from the outset between all member states that simply adding new member state nationals on to the existing complement of Community officials would lead to an excessively inflated bureaucracy with substantially increased budgetary costs. So a "golden handshake" scheme was set up to persuade nationals from the Six to leave, with Emile Noel firmly in charge of this difficult and at times painful process. His interest was to get the less good officials out and to avoid the best ones leaving; and he had to ensure roughly proportionate impact between the different nationalities.

Thereafter we had to fit our candidates into the slots vacated, or alternatively to juggle those slots until a suitable match between available candidate and available job could be achieved. It was rather like a game of three-dimensional chess and it was every bit as frustrating and time consuming. I would not claim that the results were in every case satisfactory but, six months after we joined, the process was more or less complete; and I was able to ensure that recruitment below head of division level was de-politicised and placed firmly in the hands of the different departmental heads in the Commission (director-generals) thus frustrating the prevalent tendency among *chefs de cabinet* each to try to run their own national patronage system down to the lowest level of appointment. …

Christopher Soames was a Vice-President of the Commission and, in the allocation of portfolios that took place in the first week of the new Commission, became responsible for external relations. The earmarking for him of this portfolio was the result of an Anglo-French inter-governmental deal which the new (French) President of the Commission, Francois-Xavier Ortoli, scrupulously honoured. (…) In the absence at that time of even the first vestiges of a Common Foreign and Security Policy, external relations meant effectively external trade policy … Soames' qualities of leadership, and of loyalty to those who worked for him, together with his ebullient sense of humour, also stood him in good stead with the generally highly talented group of officials in DGI. As a steady flow of the records of his conversations with ministers and ambassadors from third countries began to percolate around the department - a British practice hitherto unknown in the Commission - a genuine team effort to fashion the external policies of the enlarged Community, a very different entity to the Community of Six with more extensive worldwide interests and greater weight in trade policy negotiations, began to take shape.

Michael Jenkins

The birth of the Regional Development Fund[3]

In January 1973, one of the two British Commissioners, George Thomson, arrived in Brussels together with Christopher Soames, the leading British Commissioner and a Vice-President of the Commission. Each Commissioner had already chosen their personal staff, mainly from a political, media or civil service background. In the case of Thomson, he had picked Gwyn Morgan, who had come up through the Labour Party machine, as his *chef de cabinet* and the FCO had nominated me as his deputy.

On our arrival it became clear that the management of the European Commission was dominated by the French civil service. The President of the Commission, Francis Ortoli (a former Minister of Finance) and his staff were French; the Secretary General of the Commission was a Frenchman (Emile Noel); and the key portfolio for the disbursement of EC aid was in the hands of a Frenchman. Moreover, numerous able French *fonctionnaires* were scattered across the directorates-general: a posting to Brussels was regarded by the French administration as a promotion, but whereas the then British Prime Minister, Edward Heath, did his best to have the same principle accepted by Whitehall, he never succeeded in prevailing on the inward-looking Whitehall culture.

The first task of the new Commission was to divide out the portfolios among the arriving Commissioners. At this point, Thomson ran into an obstacle. At a summit meeting in December of the previous year between Heath and Pompidou, the principle of the creation of a regional development fund focused on industrial decline within the EC had been agreed at least in part to balance the large subsidies destined for the agricultural sector in France. However, Ortoli and his staff made a determined effort to allocate responsibility for regional development outside British hands within the Commission and a great deal of high level communication between Brussels, Paris and Whitehall was required to secure the responsibility for regional policy with ourselves. Indeed, the French turned the issue of the Regional Development Fund into an Anglo-French battle where, far from seeing the fund as some form of compensation for the contributions which Britain was due to make under the CAP, they sought a share of the fund equivalent to that of Britain and to this end they ultimately prevailed on a reluctant Thomson to agree that the fund should be divided between the member states on the basis of quotas rather than of needs.

---

3   Michael Jenkins wrote this article very shortly before his death on 31 March 2013

Thomson was fortunate in that the director-general within the Commission responsible for the creation of a regional policy was an energetic and creative Italian diplomat, Renato Ruggiero (who subsequently became Italy's ambassador to the EC and, briefly, Italy's Foreign Minister). With the early departure of Gwyn Morgan from the Cabinet for health reasons, I became the *chef de cabinet*, and Ruggiero and I worked closely together on proposals which were agreed by the Commission and then negotiated within the Council of Ministers. This process took up the major part of the four years of Thomson's EC mandate, and was a dogged fight all the way. In the Council, a German minister, Hans Apel, on realising the size of the German net contribution to the proposed Regional Fund, went so far as to describe it as deferred "war reparations."

One administrative innovation to which the British needed to adapt was that of the *cabinet* or personal staff surrounding each Commissioner, acting as his daily source of information and the enforcer of his policies. Independent of the directorates-general, the *cabinet* was a vital cog in the bureaucratic chain, and by working effectively with the director-general on the one hand, and the Commission on the other, could contribute significantly to the conception and execution of policy to an extent that a private office in London, staffed by civil servants and one or two political advisers focused on party or media affairs, is unable to do. The *cabinet* system also enabled Commissioners to take a collective interest in the work of their colleagues so that they could contribute meaningfully to discussion at the weekly meetings of the Commission. In the case of Thomson, there was an occasion when he precipitated a massive row by successfully challenging an aid project, known as President Bongo's Railway, sponsored by the French Aid Commissioner Claude Cheysson which was a purely "pork barrel" handout to the President and his ministers in the Gabon. This episode was a vivid illustration of the jealous way in which France administered community aid within her former colonial territories.

The French had been accustomed to having their way in the Commission and viewed the arrival of the British as a challenge. For our part, this was a challenge which we were ready to take on and after a number of months where each party was only too ready to doubt the motivations of the other, we became accustomed to working as colleagues. Commissioners and senior officials of other nationalities appeared content with a state of affairs which, until major issues subsequently arose, enabled the Commission to operate in relative harmony. Real battle was only joined in 1978, in both the Commission and the Council, when the then President, Roy Jenkins (for whom I was by then working as Senior Adviser), asked me to devise a two-year solution to the question of the large and growing net British contribution to the EC budget: this proved to be a far more enduring issue – a true "three-pipe problem" - but that is another narrative.

Christopher Audland

Modernising the Commission's Services

From the moment of British Accession to the European Communities, I longed to be appointed to the Commission staff. Why? Because I had been convinced, once Robert Schumann had made his historic Declaration, on 9 May 1950, that it was in the interest of Europe as a whole, including Britain, to move towards a federal system, limiting the freedom of manoeuvre of individual Nation States, which had so often, over the centuries, led to war; and I wanted to serve that great cause.

In the late 1940's and early 1950's, I had come to know many of the Founding Fathers, and had watched the Great Debates on European integration in the Council of Europe Assembly. Early in the 1960's, I had personally written MacMillan's application for UK membership of the Communities; and then - with that great European, the late John Robinson - served as one of the twin work-horses of Ted Heath's negotiating team. After De Gaulle's veto, I moved to other work, and by 1973 was serving as a British Diplomat in Bonn. There, I learnt that the British Government wanted me to be appointed as Deputy to the Commission's incredibly able Secretary-General, Emile Nöel, whom I had known personally for two decades.

In Brussels for an interview, Emile asked which University I had attended. I said "none". He was taken aback. The rules required Grade A Staff to hold a degree. But he was not a man easily put off. After a pause, he said: "Well, I think one could regard 25 years in the UK Diplomatic Service as being equivalent to a degree." He then explained that I would be one of two Deputy Secretaries-General. Mine would be a new post, whose creation was seen as necessary, to cope with the challenge of major enlargement. My first task would be to modernise the Commission Services, and improve their coordination. My second would be to ensure that more was done to develop the Institution's relations with the European Parliament (EP) which would soon be directly elected, and thereby gain in authority & political weight.

I found no difficulty in becoming part of the Commission "family". The old hands welcomed the newcomers. There was a tremendous sense of team spirit. And, contrary to what many suppose, language was never a big problem.

Very soon, I put a paper on internal co-ordination to the Commission. The administrative practices in the Commission Services had grown up pragmatically. There were no standard procedures for routine tasks. Each service had its own. Much depended on whether its origins lay with the ECSC, the EEC or Euratom. For recruits from the new member states, the result was complete bafflement. A manual of procedures was the obvious answer. I put this idea to Emile, who at once told me to write it, basing myself on best practice. The first edition appeared in 1976. It found immediate acceptance as a sort of bible, and has been updated ever since.

I next set about improving the Commission's internal decision making process, by organising a new form of devolution for the making of minor decisions by the Commission. There was already a "written procedure" but it was slow and relatively cumbersome. I proposed that the Commission should consider delegating its corporate responsibility for minor matters to the Commissioner responsible – so-called *habilitation*. The new procedure greatly eased the conduct of routine business.

It was also clear that the legislative process of the Community was creaking. The Commission made many legislative proposals: but often these were blocked in the Council. Qualified majority voting was then almost never used, even when prescribed by the Treaty. De Gaulle's legacy meant that the Council always sought unanimity, regardless of the legal position, so Commission proposals lay on the table for years. This was bringing the Community into disrepute. At my suggestion, the Commission reviewed all its pending proposals; withdrew any it saw as without prospect of success; and made clear that responsibility lay with the Council.

Other changes had to do with policing the respect of Community Law. The Commission was active in proposing new laws, but did not check whether they were being applied. Progressively, a much tougher policy was set in place. Machinery was established to check the extent to which member states correctly transposed Council Directives into their national law. The Court welcomed this tougher line, and almost always found for the Commission. Fortunately, member states have on the whole been good about respecting Court judgments.

As regards the development of good relations with the European Parliament, officials from the Secretariat General started systematically attending every EP committee meeting and reporting on proceedings to the Commission; contacts were built up with the Parliament's Secretariat and with MEP's; a Commissioner was given responsibility for improving relations with the Parliament; the Commission proposed that the Parliament be given real powers over the Community budget, and this happened; it also urged member states to honour their Treaty commitment to arrange direct elections, and this was agreed in 1979.

My experience in the Commission on these and other subjects is more fully covered in my autobiography[4].

---

4   CJ Audland - *Right Place – Right Time,* Durham 2004, Memoir Club (ISBN 1-84104-091-0)

Leslie Fielding

" 'Bye, 'Bye Blighty – I'm off to Brassholes"

Coming down from Cambridge in 1956, I joined the FO, and loved it from the start. I was happy as Larry – and looked good in the uniform!

But Arcadia is never forever; Olympus is not an abiding abode for mortal men. The Scots have a saying: "There's aye a muckle slappy steen, at ilka body's door!"

On the First of April (natch), 1973, I found myself on secondment as a director in the Commission's Directorate General for External Relations. Ted Heath had called for volunteers (demanding that they make a good impression by being ready and able to work in French - he of course was monoglot); my boss, whom I had thitherto taken as a friend and ally, pushed me forward ("Go in and win, Leslie"); and Vice President Christopher Soames, who had been my Ambassador in Paris and also my personal fine wine tutor, hooked me in (with the alarming words: "This has got to work!").

Initially, it all seemed a horrible mistake. The workload was massive; the subject matter largely unfamiliar and often very technical; the working methods strange and at times even outright ludicrous. Most of the time I was condemned, as Sisyphus might well have been, to labour ceaselessly to avert trade wars with the United States, to appease a bruised and resentful Old Commonwealth, and to address intractable agricultural problems in the GATT. In addition - and as an act of malice towards the then only professional diplomat in that neck of the Commission's woods - I was assigned supervision of the Commission's protocol service, and of a new unit set up to sort out and professionalise the Commission's growing but somewhat shambolic external diplomatic representation.

Language alone was a problem. To draft and speak all day in French demanded a level of effort greater than that which I had previously had to make during three years in Cambodia and four years in France. Since the French language demands facial exertions different from those required when one mutters away in English, I suffered from perpetual "French face-ache" in the first few months, relieved only by outbursts of cursing and swearing in German, Dutch or Italian (different facial muscles!).

There was an acute shortage of staff in Brussels, by Whitehall standards. In consequence, the workload was consistently – sometimes absurdly – heavy. Another handicap was the bureaucratic tradition of the Commission. Old timers used to joke that it was an amalgam of the worst practices of each of the civil services of France, Germany, Italy and the Benelux – the six founding members of the European Community.

Certainly, staff discipline was more relaxed, obedience to instructions less certain, than in "The Office". There seemed to be little or no career planning or staff training. Educational standards in the Brussels bureaucracy were high (officials quite often had degrees in both economics and law as well as competence in three or more languages); but their average ability as civil servants seemed to me to fall a touch below that habitual in the top Whitehall departments. I looked in vain for the kind of teamwork and the inter-departmental co-ordinating structures familiar to me both within the Foreign Office and between government departments in Whitehall.

As for the overseas offices for which I had assumed responsibility, they were few, of recent creation and operating on an improvised, hand-to-mouth basis. There were no secure communications to anywhere or anyone. Indeed, the Commission took pride in being a "House of Glass". In London you locked away official papers on leaving the office at night; in Brussels you left your files on your desk, but locked up the telephone, so that office cleaners did not spend their evenings making long international calls to distant relatives.

The foregoing will rightly appear arrogant and condescending. Early on, I must have given the impression of being a fastidious and narcissistic Guards officer, who had suddenly found himself an outcast, on transfer to an unfashionable line regiment stationed in a remote outpost of some insalubrious equatorial colony.

But the plain fact is that I was dead wrong. I came to realise that I found myself in a set-up which had more in common with a successful City institution, or the upper layers of a dynamic multinational company, than with a long established imperial bureaucracy. There were not a few precocious prima donnas; a good working relationship with colleagues had to be earned, rather than expected as of right; knowledge was power – you did not share it too widely. But the senior continental officials in DG I were people of marked ability and intelligence, who believed in what they were doing, and did it extremely well. These, and certain colleagues from the agricultural and industrial policy departments, possessed international negotiating skills, developed over long years doing the same sort of job, that were unsurpassed anywhere in the world. I came to admire them and I concluded that I had much to learn. Initially, they were probably less convinced that they had anything much to learn from me.

Happily, however, although it took time for my face to fit, in the end it was possible to rub noses and undergo tribal initiation. Thereafter, I never looked back. As all of us in the first wave from Whitehall had been given a "return ticket", I eventually told the FCO that I would not be returning to the fold (Pity about the uniform, though!)

The Home Civil Service

Nicholas Argyris

The culture shock

I remember posting my application form on the 1st of January 1973, and feeling that this date would bring me luck. Some months later, when I had almost given up hope, I was called for interview in London where I found myself at a large table, which more or less filled a small room around which sat 8 or more officials. The interview lasted about an hour and at times involved the panel arguing amongst themselves. I must have done ok, since I was in due course summoned to Brussels for two days for a medical and to be interviewed by any departments which had shown an interest in recruiting me. However, none of the latter appealed to me (in one case I did not appeal to them), not even the banana desk in (as it then was) DG VIII - some dozen years later I found myself working in that unit, although thankfully not on bananas! So I returned to DG IX and asked to see the organization chart (*organigramme*). The state aids directorate in DG IV looked interesting and I asked if there were any vacancies there and whether there was someone I could see. So the next morning I was interviewed by a very clever Frenchman, who was pleased to discover that I had a reasonable command of his language and recommended me to a colleague in charge of another unit, where there was a vacancy.

Thus, in mid-November 1973, I found myself a probationary principal administrator in the Commission, sharing an office with a Dutchman. Coming from London and the British civil service, there was an immediate and massive culture shock. First, the need to find my way around a foreign city (surprisingly easy in Brussels with the helpful advice of colleagues and detailed information from the Commission's *bureau d'accueil*). Second, the multinational environment in the Commission, with colleagues switching easily between languages: I was sharing an office with a Dutchman in a unit headed by a German, with colleagues from all the other member states. But there was a strong and very stimulating sense that we were all working together in the interests of the Community. Third, working in a foreign language (fortunately my French was up to the job), as English in those days was not the lingua franca it subsequently became. Fourth, the difference in the attitudes to security: files left on desks rather than locked up every evening, openness to discussions with journalists (behaviour which would have got one into terrible trouble in Whitehall). Fifth, the formality and heaviness of procedures, as compared to Whitehall, which, however, did not bother me at all - indeed, I found it quite easy to adjust to this new environment.

One or two colleagues were happy to hand over to me a part of their responsibilities and thus I found myself in charge of the control of state aid to the steel industry, which was a very unglamorous dossier in November 1973. For a year or so, there was not much to do in this area. Then the steel industry entered crisis mode and I found myself holding one of the hottest dossiers in the unit and very busy indeed. I had intended to return to the UK after a few years, but eventually stayed for 28 years, after which returning to the UK was another culture shock - but that is another story.

Graham Avery
From Whitehall to the Berlaymont

In January 1973 Christopher Soames brought to Brussels a strong team for his *cabinet*, but they lacked a necessary resource: many of the documents arriving on their desks in the Commission concerned agriculture, and they had no-one capable of understanding them. That is why I was recruited to join them, at short notice, in February 1973, as adviser on agricultural affairs.

Before that I had worked for MAFF in London, and over the years 1969-72 I visited Brussels regularly as a junior member of the team negotiating Britain's accession to the European Communities. As a result I knew a good deal about the Brussels machinery from the outside, but taking up a post inside it was a learning experience of a different kind.

The first months were exciting, for we were pioneers, working at a "new frontier". Practically every day we faced new challenges in our interaction with other parts of the Commission, other EC institutions, and other actors and factors in Brussels and elsewhere.

I was fortunate in having a good basic knowledge of the CAP, but I was often baffled by the practical and procedural aspects of the new work. What to make of the avalanche of "written procedures" and official documents for the Commission's weekly meetings that arrived from the Secretariat General? When to seek assistance from the DG I (External Relations) of which our Commissioner was in charge? How to obtain information from the *cabinet* of the Commissioner for Agriculture (Pierre Lardinois) and DG VI? I list these tasks in ascending order of difficulty: dealing with the documents was soon learned; dealing with senior officials in DG I was trickier (they were suspicious of the new *cabinet*, particularly of people such as me who were younger than them); dealing with the agricultural side of the Commission was never easy – and occasionally it resembled warfare.

Compared with the well-organised machinery of government in Whitehall, the working methods of the Commission were frustrating. In British administrative practice it was normal to share information with colleagues in other departments, and to prepare decisions by Ministers on the basis of policy briefs presented by an interdepartmental committee with arguments and counter-arguments. The culture in the Commission was quite different: information was not shared, because information is power, and decisions by the Commission were made on the basis of legal texts prefaced by "explanatory memorandums" which explained nothing.

Nevertheless, the work was exciting, and despite the problems our team could make an impact within the Commission. To a large extent this was due to the personality of Christopher Soames – a larger-than-life figure endowed with charm and charisma. He spoke fluent (sometimes vulgar) French; he drank plenty of alcohol, and smoked cigars (he was, after all, a son-in-law of Winston Churchill); he remarked that everyone on the top floor of the Berlaymont building had a university degree except the huissiers and himself (he had studied at the Royal Military Academy, Sandhurst).

Christopher was a splendid boss: ready to lead, but also ready to listen to advice, and capable – if you provided useful advice – of using your ammunition with devastating effects on the opposition. From him I learned many things, of which I mention two examples.

He was not an avid reader of documents, and I realised that when confronted by our briefings in his voluminous dossier for the Commission's weekly meetings, he was not likely to read more than the first page. So I developed the technique of limiting my advice to one side of paper (with a few annexes, if necessary). Subsequently this proved useful in my work for other politicians: if you put the essential points on one page, they are more likely to deploy them!

If you prepared a speech for Christopher, as *cabinet* members did from time to time, he usually discussed the draft with you. I recall an occasion when I apologised to him because a passage on a later page of the speech that I had drafted repeated something on an earlier page. "Graham" he said "there's no need to apologise: if something is worth saying once, it's worth saying twice." That good advice stayed with me.

In the Commission in 1973 it was essential to have French. If you could not read, write and speak French, you could not function in the organisation. Although I had benefited from a language course in Paris in 1972 at the *Ecole Nationale d'Administration*, the first months in Brussels were tough. Coping with documents in French was not so difficult; one-to-one conversations were tolerable (eye-contact and gestures helped a lot); intervening in meetings where others spoke better French was more daunting; and telephone conversations could be lethal, especially if your interlocutor spoke too fast. In my office, at the end of a hard day, I hesitated to pick up the phone when it rang, for fear that it would require another struggle to communicate. Members of other *cabinet*s could often speak good English, but preferred not do so: I recall a colleague from the Netherlands saying to me "Graham, when we arrived here some years ago we all had to speak French: don't think that you British are going to enjoy concessions".

Michael Franklin

Defending the CAP

Those who, like me, joined the Commission in 1973 found that the Berlaymont creaked. The nearer you moved towards the windows, the more alarming it was. If you had occasion to go in during the weekend, the whole building creaked. Not knowing then that it was full of asbestos, I nevertheless found it a pleasant enough place to work. In Whitehall, where I came from, your status was measured by the size of the carpet: in the Berlaymont it was how many windows you had. I was lucky to have four, and to acquire an assistant (who remains a close friend to this day) and two excellent secretaries. I also had the advantage of knowing quite a bit about the Commission before I joined and in knowing many of the people I would be working with, having been part of the British team negotiating our entry. Also, in the Autumn of 1972, the new members were allowed to participate in advance of actually joining. I was the UK representative on the Special Agriculture Committee, the body of officials advising the Council of Agriculture Ministers. Then, after a brief cooling-off period, I rejoined the Committee but on the other side of the table as the Commission spokesman. I had been used to making speeches criticising the CAP as neither common, nor agricultural nor a policy. Now I had to defend it (and lean over backwards so as not to appear in any way to favour the Brits).

Remember that the CAP was considered one of the crowning achievements of the Common Market. It was sacrosanct and talk of reform would at that time have been little short of blasphemy. Instead, with growing over-production and rising costs, much of my time was taken up with devising schemes to dispose of the infamous butter mountains and wine lakes. We distilled millions of litres of wine which ended up in cheap vermouth; we sold butter to the Russians at knock-down prices (much to the fury of consumers who didn't see why they had to pay so much more for their butter); we even forced manufacturers to put skim-milk powder in their animal-feeding-stuffs, though this was soon struck down by the European Court!

I succeeded a Dutchman, who was something of a legend as he had been largely responsible for designing the complicated regulations which controlled the markets for the main agricultural commodities - the import levies, the export subsidies, the intervention mechanisms, and all the paraphernalia of guide prices, sluice-gate prices and guaranteed thresholds. I got fluent in French with all this jargon even though my general French is pretty rudimentary.

The very complexity of the system made it a ready target for those who wanted to get round the rules. You needed to be up very early in the morning to stop clever Dutch traders exploiting any loophole. There was also lots of gerrymandering on the border between the Republic and Northern Ireland: I forget now why it was so lucrative to transport pigs from one side of the border and back again, but I do know that when one lorry was stopped, they hadn't even bothered with the pigs - just a tape recorder inside the lorry making pig-like noises!

Farmers are rarely happy and French farmers in particular were always glad to have a protest. At one informal meeting of the Special Committee in rural France, our meeting room was invaded by angry farmers: we were chased out and they proceeded to scoff what was no doubt an excellent lunch which had been prepared for us. During the great drought of 1976, I was nearly lynched by a group of farmers' wives when I went to see what conditions were like in parched Normandy. And I never did get to be a *chevalier de tastevin*, our visit to Burgundy being cancelled when the French police said they couldn't guarantee our safety!

Agriculture Ministers met regularly but once a year they geared themselves up for a marathon session to fix prices for the coming year. Meetings went on day and night, sometimes for the best part of a week. We didn't get much sleep, and it was even worse for us than the national delegates because after they had retired to their hotels we had to cobble together the next compromise proposals. It was all exhausting but exhilarating too. I never worked so hard before or since as I did during my four years in Brussels. Instead of returning to Whitehall to head up the European Section in the Cabinet Office, I might have stayed on in the hope of becoming Director General for Agriculture had not this post been a *chasse gardée* for - yes, you've guessed it - the French.

Richard Hay

Finding one's feet in the Commission

For me, a job in Brussels began one dark December day in 1972, when I was interviewed by Sir Christopher Soames and David Hannay, who wanted someone from the Treasury in the Soames *cabinet*. Would I (and my wife) like to go to Brussels for four years? Would they want to have me? The answer, a double positive. Then the rush began. Could I start in February? Only when we could move as a family, I said (we had a two year old, and another due in three months). But in a few weeks we were looking at houses in Brussels, and in March we moved. Once in Brussels, the work began instantly - I wrote my first brief for Soames sitting on the ensuite lavatory in the hotel while Miriam and our child slept (I don't think it was much good!).

Very soon, I was installed on the Berlaymont 12th floor. The procedures were bewildering. My schoolboy French was painful for others, though they were gracious about it. The subject matter was hard to understand - everything looked very different from within the Berlaymont, and I hadn't worked much on EEC matters in London.

I soon learnt some things. Council of Ministers' marathons are not fun for hangers-on. You could buy Marmite and marmalade in the Commission staff shop, but Nappisan came from the UK. Soames was a very good judge of the caption competitions that went round the office each time a suitably awful photograph arrived of him with some foreign dignitary.

More gradually, I came to see that though they did things differently, and the administration was much more political than in London then, the quality of work in the European Public Service was mostly very high. When people were recruited, they usually already had some professional experience and argued their corner much harder than in the UK civil service (where Brownie points went among generalists to quick agreements that respected the facts). That, and the differences of language and culture, made meetings take longer. People tended to say everything twice in different ways, so that like map references the real meaning was where the two statements crossed. Also hierarchies were shorter and much more flexible. As a result levels of individual responsibility could be much greater than in the British civil service. (The UK overestimated the value of their rankings compared to those of the European institutions.)

It was a big change. Come the end of the year, I was wondering whether the job was a good thing for me to be doing. I didn't feel my efforts were useful to Soames (my responsibilities were not at the centre of his portfolio). And I hadn't built up the essential network of contacts. I thought seriously of going back to London early. But in 1974 Labour won the election, and Harold Wilson announced his intention to renegotiate the UK's terms of membership. Soames got me involved in the resulting budget rebate work (he took me into the initial secret meeting as an interpreter, though he didn't need one; I was so bad at interpreting that he kicked me under the table to shut up). I started working with a number of senior officials (including Emile Noel, the Secretary General, and a member of the President's Cabinet) to find a solution. We met together a lot; I got to know them and other colleagues, and began to find my feet in the Commission. What was to have been four years might have been only one. But in the end – that's a longer story - it turned into 19.

William Nicoll

Discovering Europe

The then Board of Trade, my employer, decided in May 1972 that I was to go to Brussels to join the UK Delegation. I never knew "Why me?" and it did not know either. I had not been involved in the accession negotiations or otherwise in European affairs. When the personnel director – whom I had never met – summoned me to his presence he riffed through a loose-leaf book, looking for my card. "Ah", he said with satisfaction "you once worked in the Engineering Industries Division" – but in the pre-Davignon days the EEC had no involvement with engineering. When I demurred I was called to the Permanent Secretary's office. The Great Man said I was going. I spoke of the problems a move would cause, including schooling. The GM was a former educationalist. He told me there were excellent schools in Europe and he instanced Rheindahlen. Unfortunately it is in Germany and was for BAOR children.

At the time I had applied for another job, which I badly wanted. The Chairman of the Selection Board was the aforesaid Permanent Secretary. My response to questioning was disastrous. The Board's decision was predictable.

And so I went. UKDel was not especially welcoming. I fluffed my first assignment, which was to get rid of the Green Card which British motorists then needed to drive on the mainland. Within days I was the UK delegate at multiple meetings – APC, GATT consequences of enlargement, free trade areas with the EFTA countries, the response to a Moscow overture…

I was uncomfortably aware that I might fall behind with reporting outcomes to London and accordingly set up an office rule – same day reporting (it is now "within 24 hours"). The consequence was late night working, happily with a dedicated secretary of the profession which disappeared with the coming of screens and the intranet. I had a lot to learn, fast. I recall a Commission official whose subject was *produits mixtes*, on which he used to orate with appropriate solemnity. I never understood what the mixture was. When he left to become a French *préfet*, *produits mixtes* disppeared with him.

Back in the BoT – or maybe by then DTI – there was little understanding of the workings of the EEC. (There was not much more years later when I was involved in training courses for upcoming Presidencies). Officials familiar with the OEEC thought that the Commission was a Secretariat at the service of the member states. They complained that it was pretentiously "putting itself in the driving seat" and had failed to understand that the UK had, for example, a national policy on trade with Japan.

I made myself unpopular with old friends by telling them what they could not do - in some cases had already done – like imposing new import restrictions. (Years later they were still doing it under ministerial instructions.) I could imagine tales about my extraordinary and unpatriotic ideas being swapped in the BoT canteen. It may be for that reason that when I left British service to join the Council Secretariat I was not offered an open-dated return ticket.

After the 1972 summer break reinforcements arrived and my load was eased. But I earned new unpopularity among some UKRep wives by enforcing the 'same day" reporting rule damaging to their evening life. *Tant pis.*

Nothing much changed when the UK formally joined the EEC in January 1973. I kept on going to the same working groups (and new ones) and having trouble with my instructions.

Bill Robinson

The mysteries of economic planning

I joined the Services of the Commission on April 1st 1974. I was 31 years old. I thought I had died and gone to heaven.

I left the miseries of a strike torn Britain, where the real value of my Civil Service income was being rapidly eroded by inflation, for a job which was paid, in real after-tax terms, at least three times as well. I exchanged a long train journey into HM Treasury for a short drive from Woluwe St Pierre to the Berlaymont, where I drove straight into my reserved parking space.

I had a substantial office on the 9th floor with a large desk and a table which could easily accommodate a meeting of eight people. In my outer office sat three secretaries, to cope with the English, French and German versions of the papers my division produced. They also competed to bring me coffee in the morning. That real coffee and the quality of the food in the staff canteen symbolised the enormous gulf in living standards between the London I had left and the Brussels I had discovered.

I had been appointed to fill a vacancy for a head of division in the medium term planning section of DG II. My division had the task of building and running a forecasting model which was to provide the economic framework for the Third Medium Term Programme.

My director was French, as were three of my staff. So I took the decision, from day one, to work in French. I had a sound understanding of the grammar, having done French O level but I couldn't string together a sentence. So I took French classes every morning, watched French television every evening, and plunged into a new life where meetings took place in French.

I was surprised at how quickly I became able to follow what was being said, as long as it was about economics. The vocabulary is not large and not difficult. My passive French was passable within a few weeks. Getting to the point where I could contribute to meetings took a lot longer.

It was infinitely worth doing. My colleagues perceived and appreciated the effort I was making. And it gave me an entree into French culture that enriched my life.

The Commission in those days was a French fiefdom. The style of work was modelled on the French civil service. Their officials were of the highest quality and, much more than the other nationalities, seemed to take us very seriously. It was strikingly different from the attitude of British officials, who seemed to start from the presumption that nothing good could ever come out of the Commission.

I had an extraordinarily interesting job. I had to build economic models of the countries in the EEC, as we then called it. That alone would have been challenging enough. But the icing on the cake was that I was doing this job in interesting times. The post-war Bretton Woods system of fixed exchange rates was rapidly breaking down under the strains imposed by the oil crisis. The different policy reactions by EEC member states led to sharply divergent inflation rates. These events made it much more difficult to produce the medium term forecasts.

What I most valued at this time was the opportunity to meet and converse with my opposite numbers in the economics ministries around Europe. When I look back I find that I actually learned most from my German colleagues, both inside the Commission and in Bonn. The Germans had suffered hyperinflation, and their post war economic policies were predicated above all else on need for price stability.

The Britain I left in the 1970s was run according to a Keynesian consensus that if unemployment started to rise, it was the job of the government to stop it rising by spending public money, borrowed if need be. That policy approach visibly failed. The UK had lost sight of the importance of monetary policy, of the need to control monetary growth, and of the need to avoid excessive depreciation of the exchange rate. The result was inflation and unemployment.

The German approach, prioritising control of inflation, stood them in much better stead through those turbulent years. As a close observer of policy making in both countries I returned to Britain in 1978 convinced that we would never cure unemployment in the UK unless we first brought inflation under control. The next eight years of my life were spent fighting this policy battle.

Infuriating as the European project can sometimes be, I have never lost my belief that creating institutions in which people of different nationalities work alongside each other and come to understand each other's differing points of view can add to the sum of human knowledge and happiness. I certainly learned a huge amount in my five years in Brussels and I shall always be glad that I took the opportunity to work there.

Richard Wells

The multiple challenges of a cabinet adviser

Early in February 1973 I joined Commissioner George Thomson's *cabinet* at the start of four professionally and personally fascinating years. His warm heart and generous spirit, together with his transparent uprightness, at once won him the respectful affection of all his closest assistants. They were warmed too by the unfailing kindness of his wife Grace. What was more, he soon earned the trust of his new constituents in what were then the poorer parts of the EEC by his skilful, and passionately determined, representation of their interests. Before he came to Brussels there was not much European regional policy. There was no European Regional Development Fund at all.

When, not without difficulty in the Commission, George had won the regional policy portfolio, he asked my Whitehall department to recommend an expert on the subject to join his *cabinet*. My experience, such as it was, had been in international trade, and I knew nothing of regional policy. But nobody better qualified could be spared, and after a brief interview with the Minister responsible, Christopher Chataway the athlete, my wife and I set off to Brussels on the night ferry at a couple of weeks' notice.

The move made a big change in my personal life. I was still in my twenties, and recently married. My wife and I bought our first car. We came to enjoy many social contacts with colleagues of all nationalities. We began to eat out in restaurants, as we had rarely done in London. There were things we missed from London, but with long hours of work we had less spare time to think of them. The chance that our rented flat was located at a particularly delicate point on the linguistic fault-line taught us rapid lessons in Belgian politics.

Later, once the Regional Fund was agreed in December 1974 and began operations in 1975, I had much to do with it. But in 1973 and 1974 the protracted negotiations to establish the Fund took place at a level of high diplomacy, far above my head. Instead my work in the early years in the *cabinet* was to advise on agricultural, fisheries, economic and monetary and budgetary matters. These had been the most difficult subjects in the accession negotiations, in which I had not been concerned. They remained awkward subjects for those of us in the Commission who came from Britain, for we found little sympathy with our concerns about them, yet we knew that they were still very controversial at home. Despite or because of many changes in them since, they still are so today.

I found agriculture particularly difficult, for I knew nothing of it either professionally or (as a Londoner) personally. It was easy to find fault with the common agricultural policy but maddeningly difficult to discuss even minor alleviations within an institution where the vested interests in it were so well entrenched. The mountains and lakes of butter and other products were huge, yet the pressures to increase the guaranteed prices, which would add to them further, were insistent. Most *cabinet*s had a full-time expert on agriculture, with a deep knowledge of it. For me the voluminous documents, and the interminable meetings, sometimes at the weekends, and all mostly in Euro-French which I had to learn the hard way, were a substantial professional challenge.

A constant if distant background to economic and monetary policy discussions was still the "Werner Plan", under which an economic and monetary union was to have been established in stages between 1970 and 1980. This became increasingly unrealistic as exchange rates both worldwide and within Europe fluctuated, and the world and European economies were overwhelmed by unforeseen consequences of the violent recrudescence of the Arab-Israeli problem. Monetary disturbances impinged on the agricultural policy in the form of "monetary compensatory amounts", or intra-EEC border subsidies and taxes, designed to reconcile the reality of monetary divergence with the principle of a common market in agricultural produce. I rather revelled in their complexities, because my education had been in mathematics.

Though this was not a period of glory for the European Commission it was of absorbing interest to me to occupy at least a second-row seat in its conclave. And now, at long last, the Regional Fund which George Thomson established has, together with the other European Structural and Cohesion Funds, come to rival in size the EU's agricultural subsidies; and has for many member states if no longer for Britain come to represent a principal benefit of membership of the Union.

The lawyers

Francis Jacobs

Memories of the European Court of Justice

Although I had long been interested in the European Community (as long ago as 1961 my first choice for my doctoral thesis, not pursued, was the impact of future UK membership on sovereignty), in 1972 I found my job at the Court of Justice by, as is often the case, a chapter of accidents. Three years earlier, when teaching at LSE, I was asked to call in at the Foreign Office to meet a Dr Golsong from the Council of Europe, who invited me to spend some months in Strasbourg under a new scheme *for professeurs stagiaires* (or as I called it "stage professors"). I went to Strasbourg and stayed for some three years, much of that time having the good fortune to work on cases before the European Commission of Human Rights. In 1972, in common with other Brits at the Council of Europe, I was interested in transferring to the EC on UK accession. Guidance came again from the Foreign Office Legal Advisers, suggesting the post of *référendaire* at the Court of Justice in Luxembourg – of which I confess that I knew very little. I was selected at interview, perhaps because, coming from the Council of Europe, I knew something about "Europe" and I had some French – French being then, as now, the sole working language of the Court of Justice.

I had no idea what to expect on arrival in Luxembourg on 15 November 1972, but I spent the first weeks in an empty suite of offices in the newly constructed Court building on the Kirchberg plateau outside the city of Luxembourg, arranging for the arrival of the UK Advocate General, Jean-Pierre Warner, and reading the Court law reports in French. One of my early tasks, together with Andrew Durand, *référendaire* to the UK judge Lord Mackenzie Stuart and with Dwyer, the head of the very small English translators' team, was to recruit, with the help of the Civil Service College at Basingstoke, a large team of legally qualified translators who would translate the entire past case-law (1952-1972) into English for publication as the European Court Reports. We were fortunate to recruit some excellent translators in this way.

The real job of *référendaires* was to prepare cases for the member of the Court to whom they were attached; in those days there was one per member; now there are three or four. However J-P Warner's approach was unusual. He took immediately to the function of Advocate General, although it has no analogy in English law or any common-law system. The Opinion of the Advocate General reads, to the common lawyer, very much like a judgment – much more so than the subsequent judgment of the Court, which has to be signed by all the judges, with no dissenting or separate opinions, and may therefore sometimes represent the highest common factor – or should it be the lowest common denominator? The Opinions of the Advocates General – there were four AGs in that period, one assigned to each case - are published with the Court's judgments in the Court reports, and are often cited even where they are not followed in the judgment. But in preparing his Opinions, J-P Warner relied little on his *référendaire*: he liked when possible to do all the spade-work himself and to produce a very final-looking draft on which he invited my comments. His work was invariably superb and I found it difficult to be useful. Indeed I had much time for my own writing. J-P and his wife Sylvia were also wonderfully hospitable, and another (enjoyable) duty for me and another member of his staff (Susan: we married in 1975) was to enjoy their hospitality and help to entertain their friends.

Dinner parties were usually enjoyable – and one which was particularly memorable was given by the British Ambassador for the UK delegation attending the ceremonies at the Court for the enlargement of the Community and the opening of the Court's new building. The delegation was led by the then Lord Chancellor, Lord Hailsham, who enlivened the dinner party in many ways, including the singing of the Marseillaise in an unusual English version.

The Court was in those days a relatively small institution and the *référendaires* had the privilege of good relations both with the members of the Court and with the staff. There was a good social life with colleagues from many different backgrounds, from the then nine member states and from Norway: some Norwegians stayed on after the narrow negative vote in the referendum, and it was sad when they finally departed. The members of the Court were helpful: I recall interviews with several, in the course of which one (Judge Kutscher, Germany) offered me the use of his apartment while I was house-hunting, while another (Judge Pescatore, Luxembourg) gently explained the differences between the approach to interpretation by the Court of Justice and the methods used by English courts.

J-P Warner, in his Opinions as Advocate General, frequently used principles derived from English law, and as might be expected, these were sometimes influential, sometimes not. Overall the differences between the "common law" and the "civil law" systems were perhaps less pronounced than might have been expected. However, even after forty years there is still some way to go before the work of the European Court of Justice is fully understood in the United Kingdom.

Michael Hardy

Facing the challenges of European law

Before going to Brussels in 1973, I was working in the UN legal service in New York. I had long been keen on the European venture and managed to get my name on the A3 list prepared by the UK. The Commission made a selection from this and I was appointed as a Legal Adviser in the Legal Service.

Settling down in Brussels itself was fairly painless. There were lots of houses and apartments available. The pay and allowances were satisfactory if elaborately incomprehensible (as they remain). The British community made itself at home. The Madrigal Singers, the Gilbert and Sullivan Society, Burns Night – those present at the creation will remember the period well. A special preoccupation was the European School which had not had an English section before. How would this work? Attention became centred on the European *Bac*, and securing its acceptance as equal to A Levels at the appropriate grades. This was important, probably the most important achievement the first generation of Brits left to the daily lives of their successors.

The centre piece was of course the Commission and the other EC bodies. An element that now seems clearer with hindsight is that this was a relatively young institution, finding its way as it went. It had already gone through several traumas: the three Communities had been fused and there had been the French "empty chair" in the 1960s which had left its mark. I remember one official telling me how he had moved to a smaller house as a precaution during the French episode. But it was a resilient institution. Commission man (and it mostly was a man) was self-assertive, quick in argument, ever keen to seize an opportunity in the Council. Action was the watchword, and "let's do the paperwork afterwards". Shortly after arrival I remember asking my colleague Luigi Boselli for the file on a particular topic. "File!" he laughed. "For years we've been too busy to have proper files. We've always said, Ah, when the British come, then we'll have files." The result was that every Commission official had his own files and I daresay still has.

Preparing notes and opinions in the Legal Service involved studying EC legislation and ECJ judgements. It was striking how foreign, not to say continental it all was, and indeed specifically French. French was not only the working language, the Commission thought French. Perhaps because of de Gaulle but above all because of the calibre of the French civil servants sent to Brussels, notably those from the *Conseil d'Etat*, EC legal thinking, the concepts and the way EC legislation was written (all those *considerants*) were based on French models. The forerunners and precedents were to be found in French official documents and reflected the way the Paris ministries ran their affairs. It was and remains an impressive model.

Growing used to the method of arguing, the greater accent on the aim and underlying idea as opposed to the more narrowly based, strict constructionist approach of English law, was one of the pleasures and challenges of the job. One learnt over the years how to operate on both levels so to speak, how to pitch one's case. The head of the Legal Service external relations team was Jean Groux (*Enarque, Conseil d'Etat*, Chaban Delmas *cabinet*); I do not think I ever worked with a quicker, more incisive mind. We got on well though no note I drafted in French ever reached his mandarin standards.

1973 marked an important stage in the development of EC external relations. The EC now had nine member states and there was a wish to play a larger role in the world, captained by Sir Christopher Soames who had the external relations dossier. There were major legal developments to support the process. The common commercial policy had come into effect that year, bringing this area within EC "competence" as we learnt to say. But how far did this extend and would third states accept this? The battles needed to be fought in each domain. There was in addition the AETR doctrine which, in a nutshell, said that the member states could not make treaties which would have the effect of blocking action at EC level; as a further corollary, the EC acquired a parallel external competence as it adopted internal rules. The application of these two elements, common commercial policy and the AETR jurisprudence, occupied my years in the Legal Service, the drivers of our efforts to establish the EC's place in the wider world.

My work in the external relations team covered a mixture of topics, from export credits (masterminded by Liliana Archibald and Sabine Jacobs, with supervision from Richard Hay in the Soames Cabinet) where we scored a significant success in the Court (the Local Costs case), to international commodity agreements (rubber, tin, zinc etc.) and food aid arrangements. The Council of Europe agreements on the transport of animals and veterinary standards, to which the EC was a party, were a hot potato, liable to attract horrified headlines in the UK press.

The Federal Republic and the German Democratic Republic became members of the UN in 1973; hitherto there had been a political blockage. This paved the way (and was part of the package in Brussels) for the EC to request Observer status at the UN. The Commission Delegation in New York was strengthened and reports and documents flowed back to Brussels. Going through these we found that efforts were under way to codify the rules on the Most Favoured Nation clause. This was important because the EC, like the EU, is based on a customs union with a common external regime. The UN rapporteur, a Hungarian jurist, queried whether customs unions were a permitted exception to the normal operation of MFN clauses. Since a number of member states had treaties containing MFN clauses with countries in central and eastern Europe, this offered the possibility that the countries concerned might seek the same tariff concessions being made within the EC. The defence was of course the customs union exception. But how well established was this in international law? The matter was raised urgently in Coreper, written comments were sent and a statement made in the General Assembly Legal Committee using the EC's new powers to intervene in discussions. After a year or so the Hungarian effort to undermine the customs union basis of the EC faded away. The MFN issue bobbed up again in the Helsinki Final Act in 1975, when it was ably swatted away by Bob Kawan. The episode remains an illustration of the relationship between international developments and the EU; it was never a matter just of life in the Brussels bubble.

This applies very evidently in the case of the Law of the Sea. The emerging UN consensus on 200 mile economic zones led to the co-ordinated extension of member state limits in 1977, the fisheries regime and much of the EC legislation on the marine environment. An entire directorate-general came into existence. The need for EC participation in the UN Convention, raised by the Commission in 1974, led to the inclusion of an EC clause in the final instrument. In this as in other instances those in the first wave of UK participation found themselves engaged on a voyage into new waters. The journey was difficult, uncertain and exhilarating but we enjoyed the ride.

Richard Wainwright

The first 100 days in the Commission's Legal Service

"Monsieur, je vous offre le poste." so said Jean Verges, standing up and offering me his hand. He was director for oil and gas in DG IV and, seeing that I was currently working as a legal advisor to BP in London, he presumably wanted to turn me from poacher into game-keeper. But I was also offered jobs by Dennis Thompson in DG IV, and by the Legal Service. This last I accepted, because I had started my working life at the English bar and I thought that it would be fun to plead again before the European Court.

It seemed to me astonishingly easy for a Brit to find a job in the Commission at that time. But my experience was later explained to me by Jurgen Thiesing, who had chaired my "jury" in London; he told me that I was one of the few English lawyers he had interviewed who "knew anything about anything". Faint praise!

I arrived in Brussels in December 1973, coinciding with the first oil crisis. The Belgian government banned all motor traffic on my first week end, which also brought an unseasonal fall of snow. So Brussels was magic, with people walking all over the streets and even *langlaufing* down the Rue de la Loi! It didn't last, and I was astonished to find that nearly everybody drove to work, with huge jams in the Cinquantenaire Park where they were constructing the new metro.

In the Legal Service I was put into the agriculture and fisheries team – a surprise since I knew nothing about the CAP, or indeed the nascent CFP (what I did know was EEC competition law). Also at first the Legal Service did not really know what to do with me. I was given cereals policy where my interlocutors from DG VI bombarded me on Wednesday afternoons with texts to be voted in the Management Committee on Thursday. At first I regularly consulted my colleague Jacques Bourgeois, who had handled the file before me. He smoked a pipe as did many colleagues at that time so I spent a lot of time in smoke filled rooms. Bourgeois was a Flemish lawyer with an impressively good command of four languages.

Then I was also given food aid. This was apparently a dual responsibility of DG VI and DG VIII, but in fact DG VI were a fig leaf (the only legal basis in the Treaty at the time for such a policy was the contribution it made to relieving the pressure on the cereals market and taking products out of intervention) and the policy was largely run by DG VIII. I spent congenial hours sitting in the "ad hoc" Food Aid committee in the Council, so called because the member states did not want to admit that there was such a policy. A diversion was also trying to extract ships carrying Community food aid which were being blocked by demurrage and other claims in third world ports - something with which my oil company experience made me familiar.

Before my family arrived in January 1974 I spent most evenings eating and drinking in the Commission restaurant which was then in the Rue Archimede. It was very crowded and jolly, mostly filled by people like me who had just joined (British, Irish and Danish). Leslie Fielding, a new director in DG I, made a particular impression. He was more experienced than most of us and was very entertaining from a sort of *stammtisch* he kept near the bar.

My director and *chef d'équipe* in the Legal Service was Cesare Maestripieri, formerly a judge in Italy with long experience in the Commission where he had specialised in freedom of establishment and freedom to supply services. He had just been moved to the agricultural team in the turmoil created by generous early retirement possibilities offered to existing senior officials to make spaces for newcomers from the new member states, and the resulting reshuffle of responsibilities. He was an intelligent and gentle person. He had to sign the notes that I produced in halting French. I soon learnt that they should be of some considerable length, preferably with a few quotations from Roman law for which I had fortunately kept a text book from my studies. If he was pleased with the result he would stand up, weigh the note in his hand and say *"M. Wainwright, vous avez produit une belle note qui pèse bien"*.

However I have to admit that I was not fully occupied during my first few months at the Commission. So I spent quite a lot of time playing tennis and chess with my fellow new colleague, Bjarne Hoff-Nielsen, who had been a judge in Copenhagen and who was often just as bewildered as I was by the whole new experience.

Fortunately for me the CAP/CFP produced a lot of litigation before the Court and I was made responsible for all the English language cases. So I soon got into my stride and started to feel useful. Later I moved into the internal market team and finally to competition. So full circle!

The linguists

Paul Atkins

Becoming a translator in Luxembourg

One result of UK accession was the opportunity for translators and secretaries to be recruited to Luxembourg, where the ECSC had been based and the importance of the English language in the coal and steel industries had been recognised. The need for people on the spot as rapidly as possible meant that job offers, on a temporary basis, were made personally and staff started arriving in early summer 1973. The posts were taken up by people with different levels of experience in technical translating and with different reasons for making the move to a new country. Most of the early arrivals in Luxembourg were idealists, eager to make a contribution to the forming of a strong economic Common Market. I was recruited because of my experience in the steel industry and I was known to the head of Service as a freelance translator who understood the technical background and the need for deadlines to be met.

On a personal level, life in Luxembourg that June was rather different from life in London. Office accommodation was temporary, which obliged some to work two to a room, never a good thing for a translator. A permanent home on the Kirchberg came only after countless moves from one building to another in the town centre. And all the newcomers had to find their own places to live. This was a problem initially since the housing stock in such a relatively tiny place was limited. But some local estate agents and house owners managed to see that there could be a profitable market in the offing, and a small number of suitable properties became available for rent. The best choices for me were outside the metropolitan area. As the bus services were less than convenient, I needed a car. Luckily, other traders had also seen the good times coming so, for a Common Market official, buying a car was facilitated, and I was able to buy the model I had aspired to for some years. Then Luxembourg's location came into its own and hopping across the border became the norm. The centre of town was a decent enough place to eat, but shopping was like stepping back in time to a little provincial town in England before the war, with everything closed at midday, for lunch at home and a siesta, a limited range of products was available, and service was offhand to say the least. It all seemed so old-fashioned and, dare I say it, foreign. However, some progress was happening, such as the legalisation of *concubinage*. Also the banks were accommodating, foreigners from the right countries were treated almost as equals. The Findel airfield, field being the operative word for a while, was starting to have more flights. Cinemas were showing subtitled films, but spouses speaking only English were condemned to a life of leisure.

Like most colleagues, I assumed that my contract would be made permanent sooner rather than later, but it took longer than was good for the heart on a couple of occasions and we ended up working beyond the cut-off date with our next six-month stint simply a promise. Logically, with the spread of subject matter to translate, the staff was organised into groups to specialise and thus expedite the flow of work. Because of my experience I was asked to edit some colleagues' work. It soon became clear that not everyone was up to the job, either because they were incapable of understanding what was required of them technically, and sometimes linguistically, or because they tended not to take deadlines seriously, preferring to labour over semantics and literary style (this was never allowed to reach the level of the Oxbridge common room discussions of the Brussels division). As a result, one or two were actually allowed to leave, while more translators started to arrive. There was some socialising, although the small size of the division and the place meant that it could feel a bit incestuous on occasion. Despite this, we all managed to pull together in the best British tradition, and make some headway towards our goal despite the sometimes fraught circumstances. It all started to progress, Topsy-like, to what it is today.

Helen Campbell

The road to Brussels

After graduating in German and French from Southampton University in 1968 I had planned to be a translator but in fact began working life as a disc jockey in Freiburg, translating English hits into German and recording the voice-over in German. Soon I moved to Frankfurt to translate for ICI Deutschland. While there, I heard through the grapevine that the European Community was looking for language graduates to fill posts as translators. I decided to try my luck in Brussels and arrived in 1971. I applied for several open competitions, but wheels turned slowly and I gave up hoping to be convened, landing an underpaid stopgap job in the Jean Monnet Institute for European Studies, where I messed up the filing, continued to apply for competitions and learned a lot about Europe from former pioneers, including Monnet himself on one occasion.

One fine morning, just as I was about to hand in my notice, a letter arrived from the EC Interpreting Division inviting me to an aptitude test. I had no idea what interpreting was nor what aptitude would be tested, but I went off to the test in September 1972, to find myself with a group of young graduates fresh from Oxbridge, all ready and willing like me to try their luck at this hitherto unknown profession and anyway to have a foot in the door of the Berlaymont.

On our arrival, we were told what to expect – a short speech in each of our foreign languages that we would sum up in English. Out of some twenty, four of us were then offered a *stage*. Although I had no notion of the profession, or what on earth I was doing there, or what the *stage* was, I still rather rashly accepted.

Little did I know what we were in for when our *stage* began in February 1973. Night after night, as the tortures of our training as conference interpreters wore on, we ended up in my unheated flat, five minutes' walk from the Berlaymont, to drown our sorrows, of which there were many. Interpreter training was in its infancy and English and Danish had just become official languages. Conference interpreters with EEC languages, whether Danish, Irish or British, were thin on the ground, hence the need to start the in-house *stages*. Our trainers were senior interpreters, a few with teaching experience but most without. Mental anguish was the norm, tears flowed every day and Kleenex consumption doubled. The threat of being turfed out at the next two monthly test hung over us heavily, several went by the wayside, but that was the way then. Standards were high, and still are.

The beginnings were far from easy. But there was a strong sense of team spirit, of facing a common enemy together, that enemy being the French-based teaching method of criticizing, inflicting heavy sarcasm and downright scorn on our attempts to master the art of interpreting – and never, ever, giving praise. We had been educated quite differently, with a strong sense of justice, of debate, of argument. I almost failed the open competition I finally sat in 1975 when I admitted that I did not know the answer to a question but would be grateful for an explanation. "Unheard of! Insolence! She should fail!" was apparently the reaction but "That is the British way" explained the German English-speaking examiner. Senior native Brits had not yet arrived.

I did pass the test and began to interpret for real, the little light on the console was red, I was "on the air"; it was a heady sensation. My *concabins* (jargon for boothmate) were often from Central Europe, frequently with quite heavily accented English, among them several oddballs, including one who imagined she was a goose.

One of my first experiences in the booth was with a wonderful Englishwoman, Pat Vander Elst, who had been one of the pioneer interpreters at the Nuremberg trials and had many a story to tell of those days, of the appalling working conditions (compared to what we enjoyed in our sound-proofed, air-conditioned booths), the antics of Hermann Göring and other murky defendants in court. It was fascinating stuff, and a unique learning opportunity, since Pat and others from those times were real stars, offering me more advice and guidance than I deserved in my innocent and ignorant beginnings. I was aware of the great opportunity of working side by side with such great names as Irène Testot-Ferry *la grande dame* of interpreting with whom I spent three nerve-wracking days interpreting in a banking meeting, each member state with a different system and we, armed to the teeth with terminology, struggling to keep up. Irène far from abashed at working with a raw beginner guided me with endless patience and encouraged me to keep working, never giving up.

Looking back, recalling the windswept crowds standing in the Berlaymont entrance, all kissing each other and shouting *ciao Jochen, ciao Paddy, ciao Stanley!* (Johnson, father of Boris, a buddy then and a most amusing raconteur) I remember feeling a very strong sense of belonging to this European dream. We believed in what we were doing, we young Eurocrats, now a part of Europe. For all our rather decent salaries we were idealists, we truly wanted to work with our fellow Europeans, former enemies, now brothers and sisters in arms, towards our common goal, to create a Union that would never again witness war. In this I believe that we have succeeded despite all the current problems.

Vivien Flynn

A Snapshot of 1973 Luxembourg

In June 1973 Luxembourg was a village.
There was traffic on the Place d'Armes and the Grand'Rue.
There were no out-of-town supermarkets and no motorways.
To the townsfolk, Esch and Wiltz were far-off lands, where strange versions of Letzebuergesch were spoken.

Radio Luxembourg was still broadcasting from Villa Louvigny and the RTL orchestra still had players who had become musicians in order to avoid having to serve in the German army under annexation; musicians were exempt.
There was little or no advertising; events were publicised by word of mouth:
"It's in the café on the corner". No mention of which corner because everyone knew.

On the Grand Duke's birthday we were treated to the best firework display in the world, from the Pont Adolphe, and we all sat on the grass beneath – health and safety had not yet arrived.

The European institutions were known as "the CECA".
There was no Bâtiment Jean Monnet; the Kirchberg was a million miles away.
"Going to Boulevard Royal" meant dealing with administrative matters.
Danes were more disturbed than Brits about the almost exclusive use of French.
Rue Aldringen was the Medical Service.
New recruits were sent to see the social worker but all we learnt was the location of the only (and very hush-hush) family planning clinic in Luxembourg.
The *Foyer*, Liszt's final concert venue, was the Commission canteen.

Monterey Palace housed some of the translation units.
It was not a typical turreted castle, but a modern block of flats.
Translators dictated on to real discs which were taken by courier to another building.
A typist was once heard to ask who the translator with a North Yorkshire accent was!

The summer of 1973 was hot and sunny – a state of affairs rarely repeated over the next 30 years.

Pamela Mayorcas

«… Vous pouvez prendre service le 16 mai 1973… »

These were the words on the telegram, letting me know that I could take up the post of Assistant Translator (grade LA8) in the English Section of the Euratom Translation Service in Brussels.

In 1970, I had joined the Foreign and Commonwealth Office unit which was coordinating the translation of primary (treaties) and secondary legislation (decisions, directives, regulations) with the English translation services that already existed at the three communities. English had been there from the start, alongside the four official languages, because of its importance in communicating with the US, the UK and the international scientific community.[5]

The FCO and Commission translators worked in pairs or "channels", each channel specialising in a particular subject area. This meant frequent trips to Brussels, a lot of research to establish the authentic English terms preferred by UK government departments and the relevant science and research organisations that still existed at that time.

5   Full details of the history of translation at the European Commission, which includes the organisation of translation in the three communities, can be found in *Translation at the European Commission - a history*, Luxembourg, 2010, OPEC (ISBN 978-92-79-08849-0)

Gradually, the FO operation wound down as we approached UK entry, while the Brussels and Luxembourg services started to expand. Having worked mostly on technical documents, I applied to join the Euratom Translation Service. An earlier cohort of ex-FCO translators had already made the transition to Brussels, working for the Commission's English Translation Division in 1971.

After the grandeur of "channel" meetings in the Berlaymont, it was a bit of a come-down to find the English translators were housed in a rather dingy and depressing building in the Rue Stévin. All around, the big building company Froidcoeur was busily demolishing the city. But it had the great advantage of being just south of the Sablon and, therefore, in the very heart of the city. That meant lunchtime shopping in the rue Neuve - those amazing carts brimming with fruit - or booking for concerts at the Palais des Beaux Arts or lunching in the many cafés and restaurants in the area, as opposed to the staff canteen.

Later, the English translators, together with the Danish translators, moved to the batiment Astronomie, an unprepossessing tower block on the inner ring and next to the iconic, at the time, Tour Madou. Not a great location but with impossibly wide corridors, we made the best of it. Two table tennis tables were bought, a table tennis ladder established and tournaments organised. We had lunchtime exercise classes and huge Christmas parties and strawberry teas.

Another handicap was the distance from the main library (we set up our own) and from the *demandeurs*, the people who were requesting translations (this was long before the days of email) - so we started our own information service. Our translations were either dictated onto clunky Assmann dictaphones and typed up by secretaries in the pool or typed on manual typewriters. Make a mistake and you had to use correction fluid, through several copies and carbons. Gradually, we migrated to electric then electronic typewriters, then the very earliest word processors (just 2.5 pages on a disc), then dedicated word processors - huge big boxes - and finally PCs.

The English Translation Division was the first to be given access to Eurodicautom, an online terminology database, launched in 1968, that provided translations in all the community languages to date, of words, phrases, committee names, references. Much of the material was gleaned from the old Euratom KWIC (key word in context) indexes that had been published as subject-specific terminologies. I was privileged to be asked to spearhead this initiative with the English Division and to train fellow translators in the use of the online database. The terminal was a huge box with green letters on a black screen and the acoustic coupler that looked like an over-sized telephone and was used to dial up to the mainframe computer made a most unpleasant buzzing noise as it connected. The hard-wired connection frequently dropped.

Thinking back to the recruitment process, and the texts I had to translate, I remember so well the instructions received from the then head of the Euratom Translation Service: "It doesn't matter if you don't understand all the terms or are not wholly conversant with the subject matter. That you can learn or I can teach you. What is important to me is that you can write your mother tongue, English. If you can't do that, I can't teach you." Forty years later, this is still told to translators today.

The UN
and World Bank

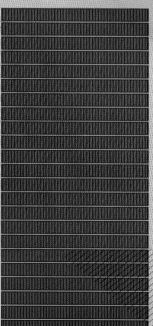

Stanley Johnson

The environmentalist[6]

I was sitting in my office in 1973, mulling over my career when, providentially, the telephone rang.

"This is the Civil Service Commission. Am I speaking to Mr Johnson?"

"You are indeed."

"Are you aware, Mr Johnson, that a few days ago the United Kingdom joined the EEC, the European Economic Community?"

I was slightly miffed. I had worked with the Conservative Party in the run-up to the 1970 election. Though I had been concentrating on environmental matters, I was well aware of Mr Heath's firm commitment to take Britain into Europe.

"Of course I know we've joined the EEC," I said.

"In that case" the voice went on, "I must ask you whether you're ready to let your name go forward as a British candidate for a senior position in the European Commission."

"What's the job?" I asked.

"It's a post dealing with environmental policy, a new priority area for the EEC. The Commission will have a special directorate to deal with environment and consumer protection. At least one of the head of division posts will be British. We think David Hannay has managed to bag Quality of Life for a British candidate."

"Quality of life sounds right up my street" I said. "How did my name come up?"

"You've just written a book called *The Politics of Environment*, haven't you? We keep an eye on these things, you know."

I was sceptical. It was true that *The Politics of Environment* had been published a few weeks earlier. I had tried to cover recent developments, including an eye-witness report of the UN Environment Conference.

6   This contribution by Stanley Johnson is an edited version of chapter 27 of the author's *Stanley I Presume* London 2009, Fourth Estate (ISBN 978-0-00-729672-9)

It had been well reviewed by the Times and the Financial Times. But I didn't think that just one book could be the reason for my sudden emergence as a fancied runner in the EEC stakes.

"Lots of people nowadays write books about the environment" I said.

"Actually someone in UKRep put your name forward. Among others, I should add. Even though we believe the post will go to a Brit, the Commission wants to make up its own mind. So we'll give them a choice."

I decided I had better let my name go forward. It would have taken a bolder man than I am to stop it.

There was a minor blip before things were nailed down. It turned out that David Hannay had actually planted a British flag not on the coveted "quality of life" post but on the "prevention of pollution" post instead.

While I was probably fairly well suited for the "quality of life" post, the job specifications for the anti-pollution post were for someone with a "strong scientific background."

In a visit soon afterwards to UKRep I was told "As you may know, there's been a bit of a mix-up and we've ended up with the wrong job. So I hope your science is up to snuff. As I understand it, they're looking for a real boffin."

"Well, I got maths O-level. Just." I said. "And I've written an article for the New Scientist about the destruction of the rain-forest in the Amazon."

"Splendid; always knew you were the right man for the job."

I was advised to get my skates on. "You have to go after these jobs in the Commission, otherwise you can find someone else has got them. Go and see Carpentier. He's going to be the head of the new Environment and Consumer Protection Service."

I caught up with Michel Carpentier, a Frenchman, who had been working in the Commission's Industry Department, attending the OECD's Environment Committee in Paris; we had a rapid exchange in the margin of the meeting. Carpentier spoke perfect English but I chipped in with some French from time to time. My French was definitely better than my maths.

I liked him at first sight. A man of explosive energy and dogged determination, with the instincts of a street fighter he was exactly the right person to lead the fledgling environment and consumer affairs directorate against other forces in the Commission. The interview went well and a few weeks later I heard formally that I had been appointed to the new post of Head of the Division for the Prevention of Pollution and Nuisances.

Taking up my position at the beginning of April 1973, just a few weeks after Britain's accession to the EEC, I would be very much in the vanguard of the advancing troops.

"But where will the children go to school?" my wife asked. Alexander (Boris), Rachel and Leo were still attending the local primary school.

"They can go to the European School and grow into good little Europeans."

Bliss was it in that dawn to be alive!

Christopher Wilkinson

Uncovenanted outcomes

Returning from Nigeria in the early 1970's and promoted to head of a (small) division at the World Bank, my then director opined that "if you want to be a division chief at your age, you are going to be a division chief for a long, long, time". How did he know? I retired more than 30 years later, still at the same grade!

At the time, the remark set us thinking, and the family took a decision that our international excursion was in principle over. The question then was how and when to re-integrate to Europe, and where to go? The prospect of UK membership of the European Community certainly seemed to be worth a try. But how?

First fill in the application forms and send them off. Then write to the Civil Service Department in Whitehall and ask for advice, if not support. Draw a blank: the Civil Service Department will only act on behalf of existing UK civil servants, not other UK citizens (sic). So, you're on your own.

Change tack: Father – then Vicar of a Huddersfield parish – wrote to our MP to ask for support for an appointment to an administrative position in the Commission. Apparently, that letter arrived on the desk of Gwyn Morgan, *chef de cabinet* of George Thomson. This led to an interview with Gwyn Morgan at the Commonwealth Club in Westminster: "But Christopher, we would need you to apply to the Commission." "But Gwyn, I did just that months ago ..."

This led to an interview with Lamberto Dini, director in DG IX (Admin): *"Monsieur Wilkinson, vous êtes relativement jeune à ce niveau (A3), mais, pourquoi pas?"* In parallel the EIB offered a loan-officer position in Luxembourg. I accepted the offer from the Commission to join DG XVI (regional policy) where I landed in May 1973. The director general had commented "at least he can speak French". I was told that it was urgent to arrive because of the imminent creation of the Regional Fund which in the event was deferred for several years.

"The Times" then ran a cute story about Britkids joining the Commission, featuring my erstwhile World Bank colleague, Stanley Johnson and myself.

Why regional policy? With my background in development economics, the Commonwealth, OECD and the World Bank, I had rather assumed that I would slot into DG VIII with its responsibility for the EDF (European Development Fund) But no.

Higher politics were in play: the UK had declined to fund the EDF (then extra-EC budget) until the African and Caribbean Commonwealth countries were included. So, apart from the eminence of Maurice Foley, as Deputy Director General of DG VIII, responsible for the negotiation of the Lomé convention, there were to be no senior UK posts in DG VIII, for some time.

So, I went to DG XVI. An early conversation with a member of the new division was revealing: *"Monsieur Wilkinson, il y a déjà beaucoup de Wilkinsons dans la Commission. Vous êtes de la même famille?" "Non, Sergio, c'est un nom assez commun en Angleterre." "Ah, non ... qui en est El Padrone?"* It took some time before the Wilkinsons's private and professional correspondents, including the Belgian banks, got used to all those homonyms.

The division had inherited responsibility for ECSC reconversion. The ECSC had its own resources, albeit modest, and could borrow internationally in the name of the High Authority (Eurobonds by any other name). So, I had been appointed to manage a non-existent Regional Fund, and found, almost by accident, that the division's competences included a subsidised lending facility for industrial redevelopment of the coal and steel regions through the European Community. Now, that was something that I knew about! Particularly as from Corby and Consett to the Clyde, we really had a significant opportunity to do something of relevance to Great Britain in regions which were particularly affected by industrial decline in the steel industry, as it then was.

But it wasn't only in the UK. We also had a lot of business in the Lorraine. I recall President Ortoli's Cabinet calling: "There is a project for the automobile industry to re-employ workers from the steel industry in the Lorraine. What can we do about it?" "Well, if you look in your in-box, you may find the written procedure for one of the largest ECSC reconversion loans, ever. All you need to do is to tell the Secretariat General that M. Ortoli approves the decision by written procedure." (*hic et nunc*).

But the reconversion policy for the steel industry did not enjoy unanimous support. Within DG XVI, it became clear that the Italian position was that regional development should not be financed by loans but rather by budgetary grants. Thus, the precedent of ECSC reconversion loans was not welcome. Also, before the Euro, exchange rate risks were an issue for medium to long term loans, especially for SMEs. The Commission demanded an exchange risk guarantee from national treasuries to support ECSC loans, since they were subsidised. Whitehall demurred. Not for the first or the last time, there was an unspoken presumption - later confirmed – that the pound sterling was over-valued.

I have not touched on the organisation of the lobbying (and the gardening) surrounding the opening of the Woluwé European School. I have not mentioned the impact of the 1975 UK referendum on the morale and the politics of the British staff already in Brussels at the time. Nor the progressive shift from French to English among the Commission's working languages. Nor the complex business of recruiting new member state staff, and organising multi-lingual professional *concours* in economics and business. All that may be for another time, another place, but should not be forgotten.

Academia

Martyn Bond

The past is another country

The past is another country. Forty years past seems like another continent. They certainly did things differently there, and in retrospect I seem to myself to have been almost a different person. Who was that tall, enthusiastic thirty-one year old who said goodbye to his wife and children and set off from a furnished flat across Square Ambiorix to the General Secretariat of the Council in the Charlemagne building at nine o'clock – as the contract specified - on New Year's morning 1974?

Just the same man who came trudging back home an hour later, disappointed but certainly wiser. The front doors of the Charlemagne were securely locked and chained that morning, and when I eventually roused a bemused security guard in the underground garage, I learned that the Council – *"mais naturellement, Monsieur"* – was shut that day. *"C'est la fête."*

I had come from Northern Ireland where – certainly in security terms – there was no *fête*. From 1970 I was teaching European Studies at the New University of Ulster, just as the Troubles intensified. Unsurprisingly, I was looking for an opportunity to get my young family beyond the sound of gunfire. An advertisement in the Economist for staff for the European Community in Brussels was not an opportunity to miss.

Fortunately, Whitehall seem to have misjudged the importance of junior administrative posts in Brussels, assuming that only what was then classified as A5 and upwards was worthy of civil service attention. That was just the first of several mistakes about Brussels made by Whitehall, but that is another story. It left the General Secretariat of the Council free to select outsiders with a wider range of academic specialisations and with experience outside government, especially at the lower levels of the administrative grade.

I sat the entrance examinations in 1973 in the Agricultural Halls in London, with rows of desks reminiscent of school and university. In retrospect, the papers were fun, with enough précis and translations relating to the *paperasse* of official jargon that was the reality of Brussels, but also imaginative questions to make you think. I recall still the challenge of writing a long essay on the potential relations over the next twenty years between Brussels and Beijing.

Working in the small Press Office of the Council for my first eight years I enjoyed a bird's eye view of everything that was going on there. With a more experienced German colleague who served as my mentor, I was spared the worst gaffes of a new boy. We acted as the interface between the Council and the media, especially when Ministers were not in town and the press offices of the Permanent Representations were not working in top gear. We chaired the Presidency press conferences, wrote the press releases, and generally briefed from a Council - that is to say a European - rather than any national perspective.

The media circus then took Brussels seriously. "Background" and "off the record" really meant it. In the early years journalists were all assumed to be learning, looking to understand the issues, irrespective of the angle from which their papers would later interpret them. All, that is, except a couple of British freelancers who lived off the scandals and prejudices that gradually gained ground later across the popular end of the spectrum.

We reported to a mild mannered Secretary General, Nicholas Hommel, a former Luxembourg ambassador, and a French *chef de cabinet* with a caustic tongue, especially when you made mistakes. He certainly taught me not only a sardonic line in formal French, but also expletives seldom heard elsewhere. He had a great respect for German efficiency as well as for the fresh thinking brought by British newcomers. Sadly, however, he died at his desk a few years after my arrival – no suggestion of *post hoc ergo propter hoc* – but more likely due to the increased workload of the first enlargement, and his growing predilection for Scotch whisky.

UKRep was headed in those early days by an impressive ambassador, Sir Michael Palliser. He enjoyed the admiration generally given to the Brits as newcomers, the status due to his office, his family ties to the founding fathers (Lady Palliser was a daughter of Paul Henri Spaak), and the influence gained through the intelligence and efficiency of his team, both in Brussels and back in Whitehall. It was a winning combination, never really equalled since.

Overall the Community was served by big figures then. I probably exaggerate - but only slightly - when I recall debates in Coreper on the thirteenth floor of the Charlemagne that echoed Demosthenes, and clashes in Council of Ministers late in the night that could have been scripted by Homer. Is it too fanciful to see in Delors coming over from the Berlaymont to the Ministers a faint image of Moses coming down from the mountain to confront the Israelites with the tablets of stone? But perhaps it is simply that we always think that they were giants who went before us, and only pygmies come afterwards.

Hywel Ceri Jones
From Sussex to Erasmus

I left my post at the University of Sussex , where I had been working with Vice-Chancellor Asa Briggs on academic planning and development, to head up in 1973 what was a brand new Division for Education and Youth which had been set up in the Commission to coincide with the first enlargement of the then EEC. At Sussex I had gained experience of working with the OECD, UNESCO and the International Institute of Educational Planning, and Asa Briggs, a committed European, strongly encouraged me to apply for a post in Brussels as he knew too of my close interest in the University's School of European Studies. One of my three interviews took place in Kensington where I was cross-examined by Jean Degimbe, later in my career to be my director general when I moved to DG V.

The new structure in the Commission was the direct result of the initiative of Commissioner Altiero Spinelli in the outgoing Commission, who had the vision to argue that cooperation in education, and indeed culture, were necessary to building a lasting European integration process. Until then the word "education" had been taboo, with the French minister Guichard especially insisting that this area should be an exclusively intergovernmental matter.

I confess I had no clear idea then of the significance of my appointment, so I was delighted to find scope for initiative with a *tabula rasa* as a springboard in my new department (then called division). Lodged in a new portfolio combining Education with Science and Research, I was fortunate to have Professor Ralf Dahrendorf as my Commissioner with his brilliant academic credentials and keen understanding of the role of education, and of national sensitivities about its place, on the European stage. The division was located in the then DG XII, with Gunter Schuster proving to be a supportive director general even though his primary interests were in science.

On the back of an envelope, sitting in the Drum (the well-known pub near the Commission) one evening, I drafted with a colleague the idea of promoting programmes of joint study between institutions of higher education. I had been influenced by the experience I had witnessed at Sussex of the success of its School of European Studies in organising periods of study abroad for students in all disciplines (not just linguists) to spend a year abroad in Europe as an integral and recognised part of their degree qualifications. I was convinced that such a project could work on a larger European wide scale. I am happy to say that this idea then found its place in the first 22 -point Education Action Programme. Thanks especially to Dahrendorf's charismatic presence, Ministers of Education subsequently agreed to launch the Programme though it was on the basis of a "mixed" resolution which blurred the line between what was intergovernmental and what could be justified by the Treaty of Rome.

This little seedling was to grow into the Erasmus Programme. The initiative broke new ground from the outset. Unlike virtually all other Commission action at that time, typically legislative in character, we designed the initiative to empower the universities themselves to be the drivers and decision-makers of the joint study programmes (not the member state authorities) thus providing the framework to ensure the academic guarantees that the studies pursued would be recognised explicitly by the degree-awarding authorities themselves. This year the programme has reached more than three million students in all, with almost all European universities involved, and has also acquired a global dimension with Erasmus Mundus brokering partnerships with other regions of the world. The basic architecture of the programme has remained intact since its foundation in the 1970s. The formal creation of the Erasmus programme with its firm legal basis as such in 1987, controversial though it was, confirmed the architecture of the programme which has continued to attract students and universities to engage enthusiastically in it and has made a distinctive contribution to the idea of Europe. This certainly exceeded my wildest dreams when I joined the Commission in 1973!

Roy Pryce

Appointment in Brussels

On the morning of Wednesday 24 January 1973 I was at my desk at the University of Sussex. The telephone rang. "Congratulations" said the caller. I confessed bafflement. "Have you not seen today's FT?" he asked. "It says that you are to be offered a job as a director in the Commission's Information Service."

This was news to me. I was one of the small group of Brits who had previously worked for the Community, in my case starting with the High Authority of the Coal and Steel Community in April 1957. But after the General's veto of our first attempt to join I had resigned my post as head of the London information office. I had then spent eight years at Sussex creating and building up a Centre for Contemporary European Studies devoted essentially to teaching and research about the Community.

Once entry became a realistic prospect I was asked if I would be interested in returning to work for the Commission and was interviewed by George Thomson and Christopher Soames in the autumn of 1972. I had heard nothing in the meantime. I now discovered that my name was in a package of proposals agreed by *chefs de cabinet* which still had to go before the Commission. It had been a tough business putting it together and a matter of luck that a particular slot had come my way. The following day the Commission approved the package. I was hastily summoned to the Berlaymont and urged to take up the post as soon as possible, and preferably yesterday.

Fortunately the family was willing to move to Brussels and the University allowed me to leave at the end of term. A friend who was also heading for Brussels organised a celebration "on the eve of our departure for Brussels ": a new British expeditionary force was about to set off across the Channel. Enthusiasm and hopes were high. It had been a long wait but we now had a real opportunity to contribute to the making of an enlarged Community. I left for Brussels on April 1st – hoping that the date was not ill-chosen.

I was no stranger to the Berlaymont, had many friends there, and knew very well most of the personnel in what was then DG X. This was a great help at a time of considerable upheaval. Many of the old hands, including a long-serving director-general, had left and there were mixed hopes and fears about the pending reorganisation. This proved to be a very prolonged and messy affair: it was not finally settled until the end of 1975. Two years later, with the arrival of the Jenkins Commission, it all started over again.

In the meantime other changes were challenging old habits: the rapid growth of the use of English for instance, and- in our case – the introduction of more informal ways of working together. But most of our troops remained committed and enthusiastic, and ready to take and also respond to new initiatives. Once the Commission had approved our annual programme - and few of its members showed much interest in our work unless they sought funds for pet projects - we had a reasonably free hand to get on with the job.

Days were long but meanwhile I had to look around for accommodation while the rest of the family stayed behind. I alighted on a house situated close to the European School (for our three daughters), shops and the Bois de la Cambre but up a steep and winding path. Our furniture failed to arrive when expected and it took some time to locate it in the docks at Antwerp. Then the removers' men threatened to go on strike when they saw the steep path ahead of them. We were relieved when the job was done and we could gradually make the place habitable. And having become used to some of the strange local habits - not least the alarming *priorité à droite* at intersections - we began to appreciate the many virtues of living in Brussels.

Nigel Robson

From agricultural economist to project manager

In 1972 I was working as an agricultural economist in the North of Scotland College of Agriculture in Aberdeen, doing research, collecting data from farmers and lecturing to students. Due to a retirement, a post of Senior Agricultural Economist became vacant. I and a few other colleagues applied for the post. However, the professor who was Head of the Department was determined to appoint an external candidate who was much younger, less experienced and less qualified. He got the job. So, what to do next?

At the end of 1972, adverts appeared in newspapers for officials in the European Commission in various fields such as law, Customs & Excise, but also agriculture. I sent for the application forms, completed them and sent them off. I said to my wife "We don't stand a hope in hell, but it's only costing a 4p stamp." In due course I was invited to London to take written exams in Alexandra Palace. In the general and language exams there were hundreds of people in the room, but in the agriculture exam, only 11 of us. I could answer all the questions and came out with writer's cramp.

There was a long interval with no communication, but then I was invited to come to London for an interview. I thought it was probably a disaster. I was asked a series of questions in German about my career in agriculture to which I could not reply as I did not have the relevant vocabulary. Then a guy put a proposition to me which I thought was preposterous, so I quoted relevant statistics, took his argument apart and destroyed it. On leaving, I rang my wife and said "Forget it, we won't be going to Brussels".

There followed another long interval with no communication, then I was invited to Brussels for a medical exam. I took a day out of the office, flying the night before. However it became apparent that this was not just a medical exam. I had to see the administration and a series of interviews were lined up with heads of division in DG VI who were interested in recruiting me. I had to ring a colleague in Aberdeen and ask him to do my lecture the next morning for me. One of the interviews proved to be impossible as the head of division only spoke Italian and French and I only spoke English and German, so we couldn't communicate at all. I was finally recruited by a Dutch boss whose English was almost as good as mine, so the lack of French was not a problem.

The letter from the administration asked me to report to my new service on 1st November 1973. I walked to the office through the snow. The office was of course closed. It was also closed on 2nd November. I enrolled for the intensive French course, two hours a day before work, and at the end of twelve months I could work in French. I also did the course in German to the same level, but never used it, as all the Germans I met spoke excellent English.

My wife and daughter came over for Christmas 1973 after Sabena cancelled my flight to Aberdeen, offering no alternative, but she luckily got a cancellation via London to Brussels. This was at the height of the miner's strike and fuel restrictions, so she was glad to leave the UK.

I worked over the years with some excellent colleagues, and it was a great experience. I became a head of division myself but did not really enjoy all the administrative work, writing staff reports (on one occasion for two Divisions as I was managing both at the same time), and the general hassle from all and sundry. In the end I caused some very raised eyebrows by resigning early, and left the Commission in December 1998.

I immediately found other work managing research projects for DG XIII on a part time basis, but that took me to many places in Europe, some of which I had never been to before. I now live on a small farm in North Yorkshire, walk dogs with my wife, garden and use a 1955 grey Ferguson tractor which I restored to showroom condition. Some change from working in the European Commission.

George Wedell

The learning curve

I was Professor of Adult Education and Director of Extra Mural Studies in the University of Manchester when I was approached in 1973 about a post as director in the European Commission and discussed the prospects with Michael Shanks who had been proposed as Director General for Social Affairs.

Jean Degimbe, who at that time was an advisor to one of the francophone Commissioners, put me through an interview. The difficulty over my appointment as a director arose from the fact that there was only one post available and Michael Shanks had promised this to the only Trade Unionist who was willing to come to Brussels at that time.

I agreed to go in as the head of the Employment Policy Division in the hope that matters would be regularised after my appointment. In the event that only happened after my retirement nine years later.

My directorate-general had been an entirely francophone organisation until my appointment: the retiring Belgian director general was quite incapable of working in another language, so I began the long process of improving my school certificate French. Much could be said about my early months but four aspects stand out for me:

- The importance of handshakes. I decided to shake hands with everybody, including the porters and that stood me in good stead.

- The relationships "the services" had with the Commissioner's cabinet. The work of each directorate general was done by carefully selected and qualified civil servants. This was occasionally nullified by the more political interests of the Commissioner's *cabinet*.

- Of course we had the task of working for the interest of the Community as a whole. Our colleagues were used to taking account of national priorities alongside the Community interest. So the learning curve of marrying these two objectives was quite steep.

- In our dealings with the member states, we tried to be even-handed; although special arrangements had to be agreed because of the difficult conditions in Italy, south of Rome.

The Scientists

George Helcké
Very early days

By the time the first wave of British recruits arrived at Ispra's Joint Research Centre (JRC), I had already been there for ten years. "It's amazing how well you still speak English after all this time," said one young lady on first meeting me. I suppose ten years seemed such a very long time to someone in her mid-twenties. This way of thinking also meant that the new and mostly young arrivals tended to refer to the existing personnel as "the old timers" - and, privately, I rather suspected, as "the old fogies". I had reached the venerable age of 36 by then.

My recruitment to Euratom - as it was then known - came when, in 1962, they were looking for another specialist in Magnetic Resonance (MR). This was a relatively new field, so that the number of people qualified in it was correspondingly small. The MR Service had already engaged specialists from Germany, France and Belgium but needed one more, preferably of a different nationality. Since it was generally believed that the UK would shortly be joining the EEC, the search was extended to Britain where I happened to be writing my Ph.D. thesis at Keele, then one of the world's leading MR labs.

The service chief came to see my supervisor who introduced us. The upshot was that, notwithstanding General De Gaulle's "Non", the following year found me standing outside the entrance to Euratom, on the day my one year contract was due to begin - unable to get in! The Centre was closed for May Day and no one had thought to tell me.

The year passed quickly for me. I ordered the equipment I would need and, whilst I waited, and waited, for it to arrive, involved myself in the research being carried out by my colleagues. I also returned to England for my wedding and brought my wife back with me.

At week-ends we explored the area, beginning a love affair with it which survives to this day. However, during the week, my wife was starting to miss her old job as an English teacher in a grammar school and was anxious to find something to do, a problem which faced many of the wives arriving in 1973. She was eventually asked to give English lessons to people in the Centre but it was only some years later, after my contract was extended, that she found truly satisfying employment teaching English literature in a girls' high school run by nuns. To have done the same work in an Italian state school would have meant taking examinations in English at an Italian university! *Che vergogna!*

At work my apparatus finally arrived and a new and exciting research project was decided upon which would continue for some years. Someone had to be recruited to take charge of the project, so a post was advertised and, since I was already deeply involved in the work, I got the job and became a permanent official.

The years 1963 -73 were troubled ones for the JRC and it seemed that the Centre could close at any time. However, my work was allowed to continue and very interesting results started to come from the experimental set-up - unique in Europe.

Post '73 my daughter was nearing school age and many of the British had school age children too but the European School had no English Section. I contacted the UK Department of Education and a senior inspector was sent out to discuss the situation. He needed to know not only how many children were ready to attend an English section but how many there were likely to be in the future. Rather embarrassingly, I had to question the new arrivals as to their plans for a family. The figures I obtained convinced him that there was sufficient demand and a teacher was appointed. What a class she had! There were only 5 or so children with mother-tongue English. Of the rest, some had English speaking fathers, whilst others spoke no English at all, there being two Israelis and a Japanese and, to add to the confusion, ages ranged from five to ten. This notwithstanding, she did a magnificent job in that crucial first year.

The rapidly expanding section went through several minor and one major crises which, as class representative, I had to sort out but it survived and is now, I understand, the largest in the school.

Edward Whitehead
A False Start in European Science

My European career, a *parcours* unusual among both officials and scientists, started not in 1973 but in 1964. I then responded to a job advertisement in *Nature* for an "enzymologist" to work in Paris on a "joint programme of research of Euratom, INA and INRA" into the "biochemical genetics" of yeast. Though I knew little of biochemical genetics and less of yeast, and had only hazy notions of Euratom, I did have some idea where Europe was, which was doing quite well for a British scientist at that date. At that time, Europe was not on our horizon. No one dreamt of going there for work, nor was the possibility much on offer. The desired destination of British, and indeed continental, scientists was always the USA – temporarily or permanently. That European scientific collaboration and exchange has become the rule rather than the exception is a radical change seen in my time, one for which the EC can claim credit, even if the road there, mine certainly, was distinctly bumpy. Another big change since the 1960's is the imbalance between the strength of science in the UK and that on most of the continent. The scientific staff recruited for this Paris project consisted of three Brits (though two did not last long), the same nationality for that matter as the then director of Euratom's Radiobiology Programme. Despite the UK not being in Euratom, the programme recruited the people considered best for the research.

My experience was of *total* immersion such as probably no longer occurs to the same extent. It certainly does not happen these days in a posting to Brussels – this I can confidently affirm, having experienced that myself at a much later date. There – I don't know how much you all appreciate - you are part of a recognised and prestigious organisation with a defined mission surrounded by colleagues of the same organisation, a common ethos, compatriots and benefit from all sorts of support in a city with a European vocation. Back then, I was in Paris, with a small Euratom team within a French research institute. My colleagues and I were detached from the institutions, in a new different world of language, customs and attitudes, requiring the development of a total self-reliance. Things now taken for granted and trivial were inexistent, particularly the ease and instantaneity of communication - back then just a phone call abroad, for work or private, was cumbersome and infrequent. It really was expatriation.

I had been appointed as a European ("scientific") official. This status hadn't been a particular ambition of mine. What I wanted was to do research. My daily reality and horizon was that of life in the local French laboratory, and there was in fact little contact, interest, information or assistance from the wider Euratom community. Relations scientific and political too complex to explain here between fundamental research and radiation risks resulted in me spending my career in laboratories that actually knew little and cared less about radiobiology.

The main Euratom research effort was in the different centres of the Joint Research Centre (such as Ispra). Radiation biology research had been rather broadly conceived and set up on a different model, that of contracts with universities and research institutes all over the EC. This was among the seeds of Europe's (not only the EU's) present large scale research support programmes. But one of the seeds that fell on what proved stony ground was the wheeze of sprinkling European scientific officials individually and piecemeal into contracting research centres, a hundred or so mostly recruited in a short time in the early sixties and not much thereafter. Permanent secondment as a kind of foreign guest attached to another organisation is a pretty unworkable recipe and caused great frictions for all the *fonctionnaires detachés et isolés* (apt enough denomination).

The secondment model was already in crisis, like the whole of Euratom in fact, by the later sixties. It was unsatisfactory to the contractors who, apart from embarrassing comparisons with local salaries, would have preferred to take the money directly, while the programme management in Brussels was more concerned about relations with the mass of contractors than with a handful of staff. The limping secondment model was slowly wound down, though some of us resisted as long as possible as our lives and our possibilities of being active in scientific research depended on it.

After a scientific life spent in the Institut National Agronomique, Paris, the International Laboratory of Genetics and Biophysics, Naples, and the Institute of Biological Chemistry, Rome University, I was eventually reincarnated in what was considered a more useful function as administrator of scientific programmes in Brussels. The view I got of science from both sides of what can be a deep divide - scientists/administrators - is another story.

However, the original idea of a kind of widespread European Scientific Civil Service was a start, even if a false start, towards a coherent European scientific community and research programmes that were later achieved through other means, less supranational and more in accord with "subsidiarity".

Illustrations

Prime Minister Edward Heath signs the UK Accession Treaty, January 1972,

with Sir Alec Douglas-Hume and Geoffrey Rippon (Martin Vasey is standing top right)

The flags of the Nine outside
the Council's Charlemagne building

The European Commission in January 1973:
clockwise around the table, from George Thomson
Jean-François Deniau, Christopher Soames, Wilhelm Haferkamp,
Patrick Hillery, Albert Borschette, Pierre Lardinois, Ralf Dahrendorf,
Henri Simonet, Carlo Scarascia-Mugnozza, François-Xavier Ortoli,
Emile Noël (Secretary General), Altiero Spinelli, Finn Olav Gundelach

George Thomson

Sir Christopher Soames

Commission President 1973 – 77, Francois-Xavier Ortoli

A chefs de cabinet meeting 1975, chaired by Emile Noel (second from the left)

Ispra

Berlaymont

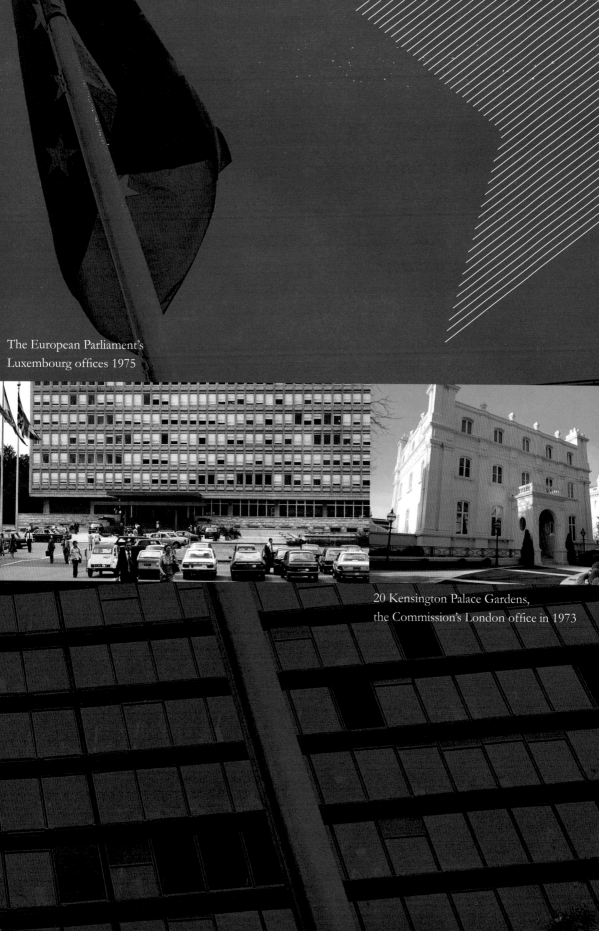

The European Parliament's
Luxembourg offices 1975

20 Kensington Palace Gardens,
the Commission's London office in 1973

European Parliament session

Michael Shaw

Tam Dalyell

The private sector

Liliana Archibald

A woman in a man's world

In the 1960s and early 70s, I was a broker at Lloyds specialising in export credit. I wrote an article in The Banker about some aspect of this which was noticed by a senior Treasury official. The British were keen to get a few City people into the Commission (Ronnie Grierson and Robin Hutton were two others). In Brussels, David Hannay must have identified export credits as a possibility for a UK candidate. So I was asked whether I was interested. I shared the then general enthusiasm for British membership, and – after one cancelled journey because of fog - was interviewed by Edmund Wellenstein and Roland de Kergolay. "We'd like to have someone to shake up thinking in the area", they said after an hour's conversation. "Will you come?". The pay was much less than my salary at Lloyds, but I said, "Yes"; I have never regretted it.

My move to Brussels, around end-March 1973, cost me a headlamp on my Porsche because of the cobbles. The car took me around Brussels and beyond rapidly (perhaps too much so for the Gendarmerie). But there wasn't much time for travel, for I was loving the work. I brought an operator's knowledge (quite a change for the staff already there). Some existing directives were unworkable; though the idea of scrapping directives was anathema, I managed to get rid of the worst and to substitute better provisions. (Sometimes, senior people tried to put pressure on me to bend the rules; the answer was always "No".) The Commission took a leading role in international efforts to limit export credit subsidies triggered off at an IMF meeting in Nairobi in 1972. Subsequent negotiations at the OECD meant that I came to know many senior officials in the EEC and beyond, which was both enjoyable and effective.

In the run up to 1974's renegotiation, Christopher Soames asked some of us to receive groups of visitors from the UK. I was allocated a group of trade unionists. I took them to Rob, so that they could see how the goods on sale there compared with what was on offer at their supermarkets, and got them chatting to customers. I made the point that the UK economy was slipping compared to its continental partners. Perhaps they got the message!

I had to learn fast how the Commission worked as an administration. It was very different from the business and finance world I knew. Fortunately, I was used to being a woman in a man's world, for there were very few women at senior level in the Commission. Staff quality was a bit varied; training hardly existed; staff management was lacking; one of my staff didn't pull his weight. But all were deeply committed to the European venture; the great majority worked very hard, and most of the top officials had outstanding gifts of intellect and enabling. This last was important, for the Commission was then – I trust it has stayed so – a "can do" place, with a pioneering spirit to drive things forward. I was also glad to be sometimes invited to dinner parties with people outside the Commission, and saw how wide contacts at senior level with industry and politics brought valuable ideas and enabled seeds to be sown for future action.

By 1977, quite a lot had been achieved, while family circumstances meant that I had to go back to London. But my new job as European adviser to Lloyds kept me involved at a distance in shaping new policies, while my international contacts remained very valuable. I learnt, too, and it's very relevant today, that while the European economy is growing, it is quite easy to get decisions to do more; once growth slows down or stops, it becomes much harder, even when proposals have no economic impact.

Looking back to 1973 from the vantage point of today, I also wonder whether the UK ever really joined. We seem always to have stood a little apart. British leaders have never really accepted that the European "club" could exist without the UK, or that no-one can change the rules of any club if they aren't a paid-up member. Perhaps now we will begin to look seriously at the alternatives, and – better late than never - really take the plunge.

Keith Arrowsmith

From Land Agency to food aid

In November 1972 when I was working in London for the Royal Institution of Chartered Surveyors -I was previously the last Secretary of the Chartered Land Agents' Society - I saw an advertisement in The New Statesman which was to change not only the nature of my work but my whole life.

The advertisement in question was for principal administrators in the Commission of the European Communities. The salary offered was attractive and I was below the upper age limit. Working in and for Europe attracted me; during my year back at Cambridge after being discharged from the army I had been a member of the University's Federal Europe Society. I submitted an application in spite of thinking there was little chance that anything would come of it.

Some months later I was surprised to receive an invitation to attend an interview. Still believing that I did not stand a chance, I was in quite a relaxed state of mind when I turned up for what proved not to be a formidable ordeal. Most of the interview was in English and I had to speak French only to answer simple questions put to me in French. In the case of German I merely had to read a page or two from a German novel and give the gist of what I had read in a few sentences.

Months went by without further communication but in early summer I was informed that I had been a successful candidate. I received no further word from the Commission during the summer and autumn and I was amazed therefore to receive in December a telegram asking me to join DG VI as soon as I was able to do so. I was required to give three months' notice to the RICS and it was on 1 April 1974 - some 15 months after applying - that I reported for duty at the Commission.

Livio Marinucci, like me an ex-serviceman, was head of the division dealing with international affairs concerning agriculture. He outlined what he wanted me to do. Some months earlier a World Food Conference had taken place. As a result the provision of food aid to developing countries had become a priority and a useful and worthwhile means of disposing of some of the EEC's agricultural surpluses. He wished me to handle this matter and explained that it would entail liaison with other donor countries and attendance at international meetings in Rome, London and elsewhere.

Mr Marinucci then introduced me to the members of his division. This included three ladies - an Italian official and two Belgian secretaries - and about half a dozen male officials: German, French, Italian and a Luxemburger. Generally communication within the division was in French. However, a friendly German - also an ex-serviceman - liked practising his English and some days after my arrival took me out to lunch. At the end of the meal he pulled up a trouser leg and slapped his knee which made a tinny sound. He told me that he had lost his leg during the war and then hastily added "on the Eastern Front".

My food aid post was a new one. There were no files for me to take over and I had to create my own job. I had a youngish Italian assistant, Arnaldo Luccacione, who had several years of Commission experience. He was a likeable colleague but averse to filing. Correspondence piled up until, with my encouragement, he carried out one of his periodic blitzes and disposed of the accumulation. After some months I had shelves of files for all the recipient countries to which we supplied food aid, from Afghanistan to Zambia.

During my fifteen years with DG VI I was moved three times, but I always took my food aid duties with me.

Hugh Burton
The importance of good management

In 1972 I had 17 years' experience in company management for Unilever in the UK, Spain and France. I could work to a greater or lesser extent in French, German and Spanish and had just returned to the UK after four years managing a Unilever feeding stuffs company in Spain

The same year the CBI approached Unilever and other international UK companies about probable EEC staffing requirements for UK nationals. In the autumn of 1972 I was invited to meet M. Degimbe, a director in DG V, at the Commission's London Office - with an A3 post in DG VI in prospect – but nothing came of this.

At the CBI's suggestion I applied in April 1973 for a post of principal administrator in the Economic and Social Committee (ESC). In January 1974 - eight months after I had first applied and when I had just taken up a senior management post with Unilever - lo and behold, I was offered a post of principal administrator in the Division for Economic and Financial Questions and for External Relations of the ESC.

What did I expect *then* from this foray over the Channel? Working on the continent was not for me novel and Unilever had its own glamour; it was and probably still is an ethical, responsible and forward-looking multi-faceted and generally successful body of companies (600 or more at that time), spread around the world. On the other hand, most companies have a blood-letting every decade or so and at the age of 40-plus…even Unilever might not forever remain my bastion. I was and still am a political animal at heart. I was and still am not a Little Englander; the prospect of working alongside other nationalities engaged in the European project - by definition political - appealed.

What did I find? The move from London to Brussels was a move from one large administrative body to another. My fears were chiefly those of being - as a UK national - a tail-end Charlie, a late-comer in the game, obliged to learn the rules that mid-career German, French, Dutch officials had over the years concocted for themselves. The net remuneration was, at the time, about half as much again as I was then earning.

From April 1974 my job as adviser in the ESC was in the economic and financial area. The world had just suffered a major oil price-hike. The Werner Plan, which aimed at monetary union by 1980, was already faltering. Was the EEC itself faltering? I began to wonder and for a time was disillusioned. My first task was to assist an ESC working group establish the real causes of the mounting inflation.

The management of the institution was extraordinarily weak. My peers fought against managing their own or any department for the next ten or fifteen years. As a consequence many sectors of the ESC were overstaffed while others lacked resources. However the ESC Tennis Section called: at 12.15 p.m. two or three days a week we drove out to Huizingen to play a set or two. We were often back in post by 3 p.m.

There tended to be natural fiefdoms in the ESC: the Germans ran industry, the Italians ran agriculture and the French ran the administration. There was intrigue and scheming - for position or promotion. Promotion by the number of years served in your grade riled me. Being the first official in the ESC coming directly from private industry was an experience in itself; colleagues suspected that I had some secret weapon they were not privy to.

As the years passed the work became increasingly interesting. The scope for ESC opinions and reports widened and contacts with civil society elsewhere in the world were established. The number of staff increased and the dominance of the founding EEC member states diminished with time. Among the many challenges I was faced with in my career, my most constant challenge was - to put it simply and without boasting - to encourage good management principles throughout the ESC.

Whilst I personally was not responsible for achieving this, it did largely happen. And by that time we certainly did not play tennis from 12.15 to 3 p.m.

Anthony Caston

With the help of Anatole France

I arrived in Brussels on the 29th October 1973, escaping from Edward Heath's three day week and leaving my wife to pay, pack and follow. It was a theatre of the absurd. It is easy to forget but in those days, except for modest holiday monies, anyone wanting to spend good English pounds abroad had to get permission from the Bank of England and for those who had no telephone at home in Brussels (this then required influence) one had to go down in the rain to the Gare Centrale and be directed to Cabin number X, just as in the films of Jean Gabin.

It was a confusing period. One of my early discoveries was that the UK Permanent Representation had very little interest in UK staff unless they had come from the Civil Service. Nothing personal, but as I was trying to deal with recruitment to the Commission I was often deeply saddened by this attitude. It meant that, for example, at a time when the UK was scraping the barrel for personnel who had real experience of working in Europe, Yvette Freschou, who had been an ADC to General de Gaulle and who was running a large charity in the UK was promised an A grade post until at the last moment it was found that she had not obtained a university degree. UKRep tamely let her be appointed to a B post. As I later found out in that fluid period of the UK entry a telephone call by the Permanent Representation to the French *cabinet* reminding them of her service with De Gaulle would have settled the affair.

The most striking positive experience in those early days were the language lessons. My twenty year old A level French had provided me with a passing knowledge of Racine and Molière and I had even read some of the voluminous correspondence of Madame de Sévigné but none of that was very useful.

Help was at hand. At 7a.m. Mondays to Thursdays in the basement of the Berlaymont we, near monoglot, British, spent 90 minutes with some of the best language teachers I have ever met. They were all good but the star was a certain Madame Mulfinger. French but married to a German, she pushed us through the jungle of French grammar at an incredible rate. Using a battery of tape recorders she seemed to be able to listen simultaneously to the oral exercises of some 20 people. As soon as one made a mistake she would cut across the recorder and repeat the correct reply patiently while conveying the hint of the message "Don't make that mistake again". Very rapidly I found I could understand most of what my boss was saying and I started enjoying writing in French although speaking in large meetings remained a trial. Periodically we had oral tests and young and middle-aged officials would jostle in the queue to avoid being next to Madame Mulfinger's door when *au suivant* was called. As we didn't dare fail we passed all the levels at surprising speed and were rewarded by being sent off to a French University for a month to obtain the grandly named certificate *"De la Langue et de la Civilisation Francaise"*.

For a middle-aged man previously confined to a small island it was an enriching experience. I was helped in by a wonderfully efficient B grade Belgian who in these days would undoubtedly have gone to university and become a Professor of Modern Languages. Madame Vidal, married to a Frenchman, spared no effort in correcting my mistakes and occasionally her lip would curl if I lapsed into some recently acquired Belgicism. One day she put a book on my desk. It was one of those large old fashioned books where one cuts the tops of the pages with a paper knife as one reads. "As you are going to have to write letters", she said, "you had better read French writers with a good clear style". The book was by someone called Anatole France. Despite my A level, I had never heard of him but I obediently took it home and read it. What I had not noticed was that it was labelled "Volume I". After a carefully judged lapse of time I returned it with thanks. The following day Volume II appeared. I am sure you can imagine the rest. I think that I can now claim to be the only living Englishman (and probably Frenchman for that matter) to have read the Complete Works of Anatole France, some 27 volumes, from cover to cover.

A little later one of my administrative letters was integrated without my permission into a training manual, to show how well foreigners could write French if only they made the effort. Modesty obliged me to point out to the trainer that Anatole France and Madame Vidal had also played their part. Unless she was on holiday, no letter signed by me left the Unit without her stylistic approval.

Many years later I did manage to gain a small victory over Madame Vidal concerning the origin of the phrase *sabrer le champagne*. Like many she attributed it to cavalry officers cutting corks with a skilled blow from a sabre. I had a vague memory that in one of the 27 volumes of Anatole France, he had laid down that it was a corruption of *sabler le champagne* and that in pre-refrigerator days the servants would go down to the river bank and place the bottles in cool damp sand. As I was not prepared to read through the 27 volumes again to find the reference, Madame Vidal wrote to various literary authorities who duly declared by a majority that I was right.

A postscript to those chaotic early days is in the shape of a photo I found recently of a very small Boris Johnson wearing green wellies, alongside my son, in a class photo at the European School in Uccle. When Boris becomes Prime Minister I will sell the photo to the highest bidder. His hair style has not changed.

David Heath

Joining Eurostat

I arrived at the Statistical Office of the European Communities (SOEC) some sixteen months after British entry. This timing reflected the long drawn out and later starting procedures for non-civil servants (see advert in national press, apply, one person (verification?) interview, impressive formal interview panel (about a dozen with interpreters), reserve list).

I was a very strong candidate: sixth form modern language specialist who had become an economist/statistician with languages and specialising in agriculture. My French and German had been brushed up to serve in the contacts my employers were having with the French and the German intervention agencies for cereals and from this also came knowledge about the EEC. However what may have been decisive in my recruitment is my name, since at this time Brian Wilson was also recruited. We always thought that the then director of agricultural statistics, a Dutchman Stephanus Louwes, was tickled by having in his directorate namesakes of the then leading UK politicians.

My main initial interviews were at the Centre Louvigny where most of SOEC was, right in the centre of Luxembourg, prior to its move to the 5th and 6th floors of the Tower block on the Kirchberg plateau just before I joined. But I did have to walk across the Red Bridge (in light snow – every time I went to Luxembourg that winter there was snow) to where the social statistics directorate of Eurostat was already installed with its new director, a Brit, David Harris. He wanted to see any UK interviewees. Presumably as the senior Brit there he felt he had a responsibility to keep the quality up.

Before taking up my post I was invited as an independent expert to be present at a Council working group meeting in the Charlemagne building just down the road from the Berlaymont. This discussion of a draft regulation on a topic I would be working on was an early introduction to the EC machinery. I made my first howler when asked to help my future (Dutch) colleague with an English version of his pro-posed amendment and I referred to the Netherlands as Holland.

At work the main issues were not technical but learning how to be effective in the strange bureaucracy that is the Commission (even though I already had experience of the varied styles of the civil service, of the HQ of a large private firm, and of a small statutory corporation). The features which struck me at SOEC were the range of abilities from brilliant to disastrous, the often bad relationships between senior staff, the strong differences between nationalities (although the caricatures I brought with me were often very wrong), and the entrenched role of the French language. I was told that it was no use trying to get rid of bad staff, it would take too much energy, that the reason for the presence of various individuals apparently unsuited for their roles was that they had a *piston*, or that they had been "parachuted in" to solve problems at home or that early recruitment procedures had been very ad hoc and personalised. I was also told that countries were generally unwilling to "waste" director general or director posts on a non-political DG like SOEC. I was also surprised by the complete lack of public files (a multi-language issue?). On the other hand however, competent energetic individuals often had great scope for personal initiative. This was rewarding at the personal level but reflected a lack of proper direction.

Living in Luxembourg was another voyage of discovery. The way we do things in the UK is not the only way, and the other ways are often better. Some aspects of Luxembourg took me into the past. The municipal swimming baths had individual changing cubicles around the pool and a long pole with a harness for teaching people to swim. I hadn't seen that since my childhood. Being asked for my *grandmother's* maiden name by my bank also surprised me. My standard of living had improved and nearly each month seemed to see the purchase of a new consumer durable thanks to the "franchise" under which we were exempt VAT. This also facilitated the purchase of a better car.

Robert Hull

I nearly didn't go: I nearly didn't stay

In the autumn of 1972, in the midst of studying for one of the very early UK MBA's at the Manchester Business School and having left an interesting post carrying out long range forecasting for BT to do so, I was attracted by the advertisement for the accession competition for A6-A7 officials for the Commission. I applied without any idea of what was involved but enthused at being part of something new. I was also applying for a range of posts in the City.

I was duly convoked in December 1972 to a very cold Alexandra Palace (complete with pigeons flying under the glass roof) for two days of written papers. Successful, I was convened by telegram to interview at Kensington Palace Gardens where I showed off my rusty A-level French. Notified soon afterwards of my success I sat back naively and waited to be offered a post.

Nothing happened and only at the end of November 1973, and having in the meantime completed the MBA and taken up a post as Director of Industrial Development with the North of England Development Council in Newcastle, was I summoned by telegram to come immediately to Luxembourg for a medical and interview. Problems with heavy snow meant getting there was very difficult and I arrived after a two day journey!

After being interviewed for a post in DG IX in Luxembourg by a rather bored French head of division I had decided the post and Luxembourg were not for me. It seemed my interviewer agreed and he fixed another appointment for me in Brussels that same day. I struggled through deep snow to catch a very slow (and cold) train to Brussels where, late on a Friday afternoon, I was interviewed and offered a post in the Customs Union Service. Following a difficult journey back, I arrived in London late and had to catch a slow, cold, overnight train to Newcastle. Struggling to bed at 5 in the morning I almost decided that the fates were against me.

When a letter eventually arrived at the end of January, formally offering me a post, a debate then ensued as to whether I should leave an interesting job I'd only been in for six months. After another very cold trip to Brussels to try to understand what the post involved I eventually persuaded a reluctant wife to try it for a couple of years.

So in April 1974, eighteen months after starting the recruitment process, I arrived in a completely new world as one of the youngest UK A7 officials. For me the culture shock was enormous, the Community structure and methods I found confusing, customs policy I found mysterious, my French was woefully inadequate but my new colleagues were genuinely welcoming and understanding. Initially I spent some time living in the Residence Waldorf on rue Belliard with an eclectic assortment of British colleagues before finding a house in Overijse. In due course I became immersed in the mysteries of customs management meetings, Coreper and Council as we forged new legislation on the inward and outward processing of goods from Eastern Europe. An induction course in Bruges introduced me to colleagues who were to remain life-long friends. I bought a tax free sailing dinghy as an essential household item!

Not long afterwards Harold Wilson announced the referendum on British membership and I joined an enthusiastic group of officials and non-officials as treasurer of a newly launched English speaking branch of the European Movement in Brussels. We campaigned amongst British residents in Belgium who would be able to vote and organised leafleting at the ferry ports in Belgium and northern France to encourage the yes vote. Out of this activity emerged the British Labour Group in Brussels and the Brussels British Conservative Association.

About this time I wrote an article on "Management in the Commission" intended for publication in *Management Today* in the UK. Having submitted for approval what was a genuine attempt to analyse the problems of managing a multicultural organisation, I was summoned by the Director of the Customs Service, an elderly German, who was genuinely horrified that I had dared to try to analyse the Commission's management approach (or lack of it). He sent me on to have my request refused by the equally disapproving British Director of Personnel in DGIX. On many occasions subsequently I took it out of the drawer with a view to resubmitting it but although it remained a correct analysis for a very long period afterwards it never was published.

Soon afterwards I decided the arcane world of customs was not exciting enough for me and I sought to move to a more challenging post. I was told I could not move until two years' probation was over but I persisted and 18 months after arriving in the Commission I transferred to DGI as the desk officer for South East Asia. It was just what I wanted. Had I not moved then I would almost certainly have left Brussels and not spent another 30 fascinating years there.

Jonathan Scheele

Square pegs in round holes

Unhappy with my job selling cardboard boxes and with little prospect of a move elsewhere within Unilever, I was looking seriously for a new job in the autumn of 1972. The Commission *concours* for A6/7 recruitments attracted me, as I spoke French and German and, above all, the European project was seen in my Anglo-German family as a "good thing".

I turned up at Alexandra Palace on a cold December afternoon for the written exams, beginning with the language test. We sat down – in our overcoats – behind desks set up in the Grand Hall of the Palace, facing the gigantic organ and with pigeons flying around in the roof. When asked to put our hands up if we wanted to do the test in French, some 90% of us did so. This revealed DG IX's lack of knowledge of the British education system, since they only had about two thirds of the necessary papers (the September 1972 Summit communiqué), while other languages were over-supplied. Someone was dispatched to find a photocopier – not easy in those days and that place – and the unlucky ones who didn't manage to get one of the first copies started about 45 minutes after the others.

Some 20 years later, I discovered someone who had invigilated that exam. She told me there was near disaster beforehand, as the team almost missed their bus stop and jumped off at the last moment, leaving the exam papers on the bus. Fortunately an even slower colleague missed the stop altogether and retrieved the papers, getting off at the next stop.

The next stage was the oral interview in late February at the newly-designated Press and Information office in Kensington Palace Gardens. I showed my ignorance about things European when asked to name the institutions – forgetting the Court of Justice altogether until prompted. In those days, merely having a degree was enough to get you a good job, so the concept of serious research prior to interview was something of a novelty.

Despite this, I was subsequently informed that I had passed the *concours*, along with some 120 others. But I was in the fourth (and last) group of some 65 people, so I felt I had little chance of getting one of the 70 or so posts reserved for Brits and I took a job with British Leyland, moving up to the Midlands. Finding a house took some time and inevitably, a day or two after we finally moved in late September, I received a six page telegram inviting me for an interview with DG III.

I had to postpone the interview to late November and was able to combine the trip with one to Luxembourg for an interview at Eurostat. There I was asked what I knew about input-output tables and confessed that it was very little, but I was prepared to learn. Fortunately for my sanity – and my social life - I was offered a job in DG III.

I really had no idea about the cost of living in Brussels so, after my briefing session with Roger Fry, I buttonholed two English speakers on the platform at Schuman metro station to check whether one could live on an A7's salary. They assured me this was feasible and I accepted the offer when it came, even if I had some problems in understanding the heavily Italian-accented French of my future director. I can remember being astonished by the details of the Staff Regulations, which appeared to me extraordinarily generous compared with those in the UK.

After waiting for some time for the official job offer, I finally arrived in Brussels for my first day's work on Monday 4 March 1974. I had left British Leyland just a few days after the return of a Labour government, committed to renegotiating or leaving the EEC altogether. My boss in Longbridge, a Labour City Councillor, wished me luck in my new job but said he expected me to be returning "very soon, since the new government would take Britain out of the Common Market." *Plus ça change...*

I got a taste of personnel policy as, between my recruitment and my arrival, I switched units and found myself dealing with the textile rather than the chemical industry. This was an interesting illustration of the Commission's tendency to fit square pegs into round holes. On the same day as I started, another new Brit moved into the next door office. He dealt with the paper industry, where I had experience, while he came from the synthetic textiles industry!

My main recollections of settling in revolve around: apartment-hunting - both my wife and I were amazed by the marble and the parlophones; Bruges – a great week, marred by poor food at the Holiday Inn but the basis of at least two longstanding friendships nurtured by playing truant one day to go to Knokke; and the Foyer in rue Archimede - where enforced proximity due to the shortage of tables also made new friends.

Dennys Watson
First impressions of a businessman

In the early summer of 1973 I was told that Whitehall had sent mainly graduates in law, PPE or languages to work in the EEC but that, with the exception of those recruited for the research centres, very few had any practical experience in industry, or understanding of the interrelationships between modern technology and existing EEC policy areas such as transport, employment and regional development. It was suggested that if I was interested, an application would probably be favourably received.

Having experienced some of the problems of marketing UK goods and services within the "Common Market" without UK membership, I had been convinced that membership would be to the UK's advantage. I felt that, with my fairly wide practical knowledge of Western Europe's industries and its main languages, I would be able to make a useful contribution to policy formulation in the enlarged EEC. So I replied, from my Belgian address, to a Commission recruiting advertisement in The Times: this was eventually acknowledged – and then I heard nothing for nearly three months. Finally I was invited at short notice to attend a medical inspection, and then interviews on the same day with three different DGs that had apparently expressed interest in at least looking at me as a potential official. Not an impressive first experience of Commission recruiting practice!

The three DGs were Personnel & Administration, Financial Control, and Regional Policy. In each case I was interviewed initially by the assistant to the director-general. In the first case I made it clear that I wasn't keen on involvement in internal improvement of the administration (which seemed akin to an Augean Stable!): I had earlier supervised an assignment in FAO Rome, and discovered how difficult it was to analyse what, exactly, the functions were of any individual in a non-profit bureaucracy! As regards Financial Control, I soon saw the Italian director general, with whom I got on well; but the scope for policy formulation was evidently limited, and then he suggested that I could be that DG's representative in Ispra – an area with which my wife and I were well acquainted, but we didn't want to make another move geographically. Regional Policy, on the other hand, was still evolving – the Regional Fund had only recently been set up; again, an Italian director general, no problem: and a German head of division, who did not consider my lack of civil service experience as a major handicap. The post on offer was in the co-ordination of regional policy with other EEC policies, notably competition, transport, industry, education, etc. which I accepted subject to delay because of contractual obligations to my firm.

I entered DG XVI in late 1973 and immediately became involved in interservice meetings with other DGs, provisionally "taking a line" (subject to later written confirmation from my director general), and in preparing responses to policy proposals from them which might interact with DG XVI's interests. This was a good "baptism of fire" for me, and I initially found the work stimulating and very interesting, quickly gaining some understanding of the political processes involved.

But there were also some less attractive aspects. Having been accustomed, as a senior consultant, to have easy access to top management of big organisations for discussions of important policy decisions (and not having Whitehall experience), I found it hard to adjust to the more rigid procedures within the Commission, especially *la voie hiérarchique*, with its *signataires* progressing slowly up to D-G level before despatch – usually confirming in writing the provisional line I'd taken in a meeting about a week before. My reports of such meetings also had to follow *la voie*. Generally, I had no problems with my German head of division (who appreciated succinct reports), nor with my director general: but between them was a very difficult and formal French director, who liked to pick holes (especially if the supposed interests of France might be affected!). DG XVI was initially under the responsibility of UK Commissioner George Thomson: but one had little contact or interaction with him or his *cabinet*, although relations were amicable enough.

I was surprised, perhaps naively, by the politization of the Commission's services – much more marked in the original member states – and the apparent need for *piston* as a pre-requisite for career advancement (one of my initial interviewers even enquired who was backing my job application!). As I had no political affiliations, and was not known to nor chosen by Whitehall, it was more difficult for me to make a desired move some years later.

Having arrived in Brussels from Milan with my wife nearly two years earlier, we were well settled in a rented house, in a village within easy driving distance of Brussels, by the time I joined the Commission: and we had acquired a circle of friends, mainly international managers of companies with offices in Brussels, and had become involved in sporting and other social activities. So we did not have the difficulties which some ex-UK new family arrivals experienced: nor was our social circle limited to other EC colleagues.

In general, I look back on 1973 as a period of enthusiasm for the great European project, requiring considerable flexibility and personal adjustment to a new style of work, providing a very interesting experience. I am glad that I took the opportunity of being in at the start of a historic change in the UK's relationship with continental Europe – even if later developments proved disappointing.

Three secretaries, and a nurse

Jo Bell

Nursing the newcomers

I arrived in Brussels in May 1973 with my four young children to start working in the Commission out of necessity. My husband had been head of division in the Nuclear Energy Agency of the OECD in Paris from where he had been sent to the Euratom research establishment at Ispra in Italy. In 1972 he and two friends had been killed in the mountains by an avalanche which swept their car off the road.

We had been very aware of the impending arrival of Britain, Denmark and Ireland in the European Community, having followed the accession negotiations keenly. How strange that I should have become part of the first intake.

I did not realise then what an exciting time it would be to join the Medical Service of the Commission at the outset. There were the usual procedures to go through before being accepted as a nurse in that service and then waiting for confirmation, but once there I enjoyed every moment of it. My English nursing training stood me in good stead: Bristol Royal hospital had sent me out well prepared. I was well received by my colleagues though many of them were surprised that an English nurse had found her way to Brussels.

Everyone recruited to the Commission passed through the Medical Service and I was struck by the excitement of it all: the Brits were there! I did sometimes wonder if people realised what a touching sense of gratitude the Belgians felt towards us. It was certainly conveyed to me by one or two of the doctors. Later on when we were moved out of the Berlaymont a young French woman put it to me: "You are not really a prestigious service, Madame Bell, we have to make room for Spain."

Prestigious service or not, we were well placed to give helpful advice to the newcomers, particularly the younger ones daunted by leaving the UK and coming to work in Brussels at the Commission. I remember being told by our German chief that an important official would be coming and that he must be eased through without delay. A very elegant gentleman shuffled into my office. I thought that he must have a brilliant brain but the poor soul was going to have trouble with his feet. It transpired that he had been summoned to Brussels the previous day and in his words, foolishly rushed out to buy new shoes for the occasion. Those shoes had worn blisters on his heels which he had treated with whisky, the only alcohol available to set him up for his journey around the Commission. I washed his socks and made him ring pads to cushion his heels. It must have worked because he was soon one of us.

Life in the Medical Service was more than just being kind. We had our professional duties of course, but there was room to speak with people and learn of their aspirations for their future in Europe. In addition to the Brits there were some truly interesting people from Denmark and Ireland whom I had the pleasure of seeing in my role as a nurse in the Commission. How lucky can you get!

Margaret Cooper
My big adventure

On 2 April 1973 I boarded the morning flight from Birmingham to Brussels with one suitcase and butterflies in my stomach. My parents were standing in the viewing area and I could see them as the Viscount taxied down the runway. I was nervous, but the feelings of independence and adventure overcame my fears and I concentrated on thinking about what lay ahead. I was 20 years old.

My journey to Brussels had begun in November 1972 when I replied to an advertisement in the newspaper – the Commission of the European Communities required shorthand typists and typists with starting salaries of up to £2,364 pa. Riches indeed; I was earning £1,300 at the time in my first job after completing a bi-lingual secretarial course at Bristol Polytechnic. I applied straightaway and was thrilled to receive a letter advising me that the "Selection Board has decided to admit you to the written tests" which were to be held on 9 December at 8.30 am at the Bloomsbury Centre Hotel, London.

The tests were held in a large conference room, set out like an examinations hall, with manual typewriters on each desk. There must have been well over 50 candidates taking part. An official from DGIX addressed us from the stage and on her word we all started typing a text. The noise from the manual typewriters was very distracting and it took me a few moments to get my fingers to work. We undertook various other tests over the whole morning. I felt very uncertain as to whether I would pass.

At the beginning of January I received a letter from Brussels – I had got through "Open Competition COM/S/C/ 101-102" and was required to attend an obligatory medical examination at the Delegation of the CEE at 20 Kensington Palace Gardens on 22 January. A month later I received a further letter from Brussels informing me that "the authority of the Commission of the European Communities empowered to make appointments has decided to appoint you trainee officer, category C, grade 3, incremental level 2". This letter was the first indication that the organisation I was about to join was a vast, complex institution. I was very excited at the prospect of being in at the beginning of Britain's membership.

On my arrival in Brussels I took a taxi from Zaventem to the YWCA just off Avenue Louise where I had booked a room in advance. I felt very important! I left my suitcase and made my way to the *bureau d'accueil* via tram. The staff at the *bureau d'accueil* were very kind and helpful and I was told that I was to have an interview that afternoon with a British principal adviser in DGVIII. He took me on as his secretary and I realised afterwards that I had been very lucky to be assigned to this post as I had little previous experience. That evening I met other new and recent starters at the *Foyer* just up the road from the Berlaymont, I was introduced to a girl who was looking for a flatmate, and within two weeks we had found a flat within walking distance of the Berlaymont.

I settled in very quickly to my new life, I got a tremendous buzz walking into the Berlaymont every morning and showing my staff card to the Security personnel at the lift. I enjoyed lunching in the Rotonde and the cafes and restaurants around the Rond Point Schuman. By mid-May I was becoming more confident and learning a great deal about the workings of the Commission, guided by my Dutch colleague who had been there for many years and who took me under her wing.

On the day of my 21st birthday, six weeks after my arrival, I was asked by the secretary to the Deputy Director General for Development to follow her … she led me into Maurice Foley's office where a large number of people were gathered and tables with white cloths were set out with glasses of champagne and canapés for the occasion of **my** birthday! Maurice made an announcement that it was so rare at the Commission to have someone celebrating a 21st birthday that they couldn't let it pass unmarked! I was overwhelmed, and thrilled. I will never forget that moment.

I stayed at the Commission until July 1977 and had a wonderful experience.

Lorna Hoe

Working for Finn Olav Gundelach

I was recruited in April 1972 to work in the translation pool from where I moved to the task force preparing for the arrival of the British, Irish and Danes. I was then sent to London to assist in replying to the job applications coming into the Delegation's office. There I met the secretary of Manfred Caspari, the first *chef de cabinet* of Finn Olaf Gundelach, the new Danish Commissioner, and through her I started working for the Danish *cabinet*.

I worked for a while with the members of the *cabinet* who were not used to having a secretary and so didn't quite know how to use me, so to speak. I then moved into the *chef de cabinet's* front office and started to do some work for Gundelach himself who had very good English (his then secretary's second language was German). I subsequently worked for the new *chef de cabinet*, Niels Helveg Petersen, who later became Foreign Minister, and when he was replaced I became second secretary to Gundelach. He had five *chefs de cabinet* in all and was furious when he went down to the 12th floor one day and found the archive girls had put *"ex-chefs de cabinet"* on the door of one of the offices.

Gundelach was not an easy boss. By this time, he had the big portfolio of agriculture and fish. This was stressful for him (and us) but he could be really charming, for example on missions. He was cultured, amusing and knowledgeable and, for example, could name all the equestrian statues in London, the history of the Danish monarchy and much of that of England. On mission - and on long flights - he had time to talk and show his utterly charming side. He was also rather protective: when we were in Tokyo he refused to let me type for other people but told me to go out for the day on an excursion to Mount Fuji.

One of my most interesting missions was when he was President of the East of England Agriculture Show which I suspect he accepted to spite the Royal Show which had not invited him. I was extremely anxious that he would at the last moment renege on the invitation as he did sometimes, but he kept his promise to attend. Gundelach enjoyed his three days at the Show as did his two sons. Everyone was speculating about Mrs Gundelach and he amused us greatly in his speech at the official lunch when he said that there was one person missing and that was the family cat.

Good if sometimes stressful memories!

Pamela Levy

Happy memories of the Berlaymont

I was already working in Brussels when I learnt that the EEC was recruiting English secretaries. I applied and was invited to take part in some texts. The typing test was rather daunting as no English keyboard typewriters had arrived - only French were available. We were told to ignore what we touch-typed and were assured that those who read the pages would be able to interpret them.

I liked the general atmosphere in the Commission and looked forward to working there. I started at the beginning of May 1973 and was allocated to DG II. Everyone was polite and rather formal - only surnames were used, no first names. When we Brits met in the corridors and spoke to each other using first names, colleagues from other nationalities looked at us in surprise. Some remarked how strange it was to hear English spoken.

Most seemed pleased the UK had joined. At first the other senior secretaries were not happy that some of the English secretaries were recruited at their level, but this did not last and they soon accepted that at our age and experience we were not going to work as juniors.

A short while after we joined the Commission an English head of division showed me a list of participants at a forthcoming meeting and remarked: "Look, they are all foreigners!" "No" I replied, "they are all Europeans like us".

We all soon learned how necessary it was to brush up our languages so we knew what colleagues were talking about when they spoke to each other in their mother tongue, or in order to stand up for ourselves.

For a few months I worked in DG VIII. My German colleague told me one of my tasks was to get the furniture from another floor and bring it back to our office. I queried this and we had a strange conversation during which I said I couldn't understand why a secretary had to collect furniture on a seemingly regular basis and carry it herself to the office. Why couldn't one of the men do it? But when I asked what furniture was in French and was told *fournitures* (supplies) I understood. I met another Brit a few days later who had the very same experience.

When the UK decided to hold a referendum on whether to stay in the EEC there was a great buzz of discussion in the corridors and lifts among the other nationalities. It was very interesting to hear what was being said since most colleagues didn't know all the Brits so they spoke openly. The Germans and Italians wanted us to remain but the French were vociferous in wanting us out.

Back in DG II there was an important meeting taking place in the director general's office and the French secretary to one of the directors had to take some papers into the room. As she entered a French director with a booming voice remarked: "Ah madam, in that red dress you look like Little Red Riding Hood". She replied, "And you, monsieur, look like the Big Bad Wolf". Ten minutes after the meeting ended that exchange was reported throughout the entire 7th floor of the Berlaymont where DG II was located.

I recall the time some angry farmers came to Brussels and for four days they made a lot of noise outside the Berlaymont and we were told to be careful when leaving the building - I was actually attacked one day when leaving by a back entrance but I shouted so loudly the man retreated. Finally, when the farmers began digging up the pavement in the Rue de la Loi, the police arrived with water cannons and within less than 15 minutes order was restored and the farmers disappeared.

Secretaries were not always treated with the respect one was used to in the UK but the majority of officials were pleasant. At the time I worked in the Commission the general attitude was that we were working for a united Europe. Most of us enjoyed our time there, making friends, living in the excellent accommodation available in Brussels while appreciating the kindness shown by local people. I have many happy memories.

The European
Parliament

Roger Broad

The Parliament's man in London

There is nothing new about a British political party tearing itself to shreds over Europe. Forty years ago it was Labour. One result was that the party boycotted the European Parliament until after the 1975 referendum, the device Harold Wilson had guilefully thought up as a means of keeping Britain in the Community and his party in one piece. He succeeded in the former but not the latter. We might yet see whether a similar manoeuvre by a Conservative prime minister has a similar effect. This time round we cannot be so sanguine about the outcome – in 1975 the European Community was a confident going concern. We could see (to adapt Marx) history repeating itself not only as farce but tragedy as well.

So in January 1973 Britain's 36 seats in the European Parliament were taken up by 18 Conservatives, two Liberals and a crossbench peer. The first were led by Peter Kirk, a determined European who died too young four years later. After the 1974 election and the referendum Labour took up 18 seats, with 16 going to the Conservatives and one each to the Liberals and Scottish Nationalists. Both main parties' delegations included a few peers. A handful of the Conservatives were still doubtful about Europe but the anti-element among the Labour members was stronger although a minority. Michael Stewart, the former foreign secretary, led them for two years. They then surprisingly elected an anti in his place, John Prescott, more for his ability than his opinions about Europe which clearly evolved over time. The turnover of members of all nationalities was rapid. The strain on the British was especially heavy as the Labour government's majority withered. The Opposition tried to force Labour out, planning divisions at short notice that led to Conservative and Labour members hurrying back from Strasbourg to vote and even rushing back to that city the following morning. At that time transport between London and Strasbourg was difficult.

As for myself, I had been in the USA in early 1964 and come back without a job. There was nothing of interest in journalism but as a pro-European I heard about a vacancy to edit the monthly magazine European Community in Luxembourg, nominally on the staff of the ECSC. I thought I would do that for a couple of years and then return to Fleet Street. But after three years I became the Commission's press officer in London and in 1973 moved over to start a London office for the Parliament. My two years eventually became 22.

Trying to get the British public and press interested in the Parliament was Sisyphean. Any hint of scandal, real or imagined, sent the rock downhill again. The Parliament's limited powers could be disregarded by the Commission and the Council, although the careful if unspectacular work by its committees in question-ing and honing Commission drafts was invaluable. In the full sessions members' dependence on interpretation made for heavy going; attempts at humour proved fatal and some idioms could confuse the best interpreters. The British proposed an oral question time session that did bring a little life to proceedings but it had neither the virtues nor the vices of the Westminster equivalent.

British media reporting depended on Westminster journalists travelling out or the Brussels press corps decamping to Strasbourg. Both for a few days escaped their respective goldfish bowls. During the editorship of the then enthusiastically pro-European William Rees-Mogg, The Times treated the Parliament with dignity. He sent a gallery reporter and a political correspondent out every month and printed reports on the debates alongside the then extensive coverage of Com-mons and Lords debates. The BBC did its duty, mainly on radio and occasionally on television despite the cumbersome procedure to return film to Britain. ITN made intermittent forays.

After the first European elections in 1979 media interest picked up but always in the background was the sentiment that the European Parliament was not a "real parliament" sustaining an executive and able to legislate in its own right. Adhesion to the simple black and white characteristics of Westminster, the "ins" and the "outs", the "big-endians" and the "little-endians", blocked understanding of a multinational, multiparty and multilingual body groping its way towards an international democracy. It does still.

Tam Dalyell

Hemicircular Politics

In the summer of 1976, James Callaghan, then Foreign Secretary, in one of his avuncular moments, summoned me to his room. "Tam, I'm sending you to Europe as Michel Stewart's Deputy, for two reasons. First, although I think Devolution for Scotland is nonsense, I don't want you, nor does Harold, being awkward about Party policy on Scotland. Second, the purpose of the Labour Delegation to the European Parliament is not to make the European policy of the Labour Government – Harold and I do that – but to make a good impression for the Labour Party with European politicians." He added with a twinkle, "Doubtless they will like your Old Etonian good manners!"

On the first point, little did Callaghan realise that it was easier to sabotage the Scotland and Wales Bills if one flew home to oppose that particular Commons business rather than being subject to day-to-day pressure in the Commons to conform. Callaghan's second instruction I worked at faithfully. Soon I was made really welcome. Georges Spénale, the President of the Parliament, was delighted that my first words to him were to say how much I admired the *Dentelles* sculptures in the fortress Cathedral at Albi – adjoining his South-West France constituency. Because my name began "Dal .." I sat next to Piet Dankert, later President of the Parliament, and then a Dutch minister. We gossiped happily. And I became a particular friend of Schelto Patijn, later Governor of South Holland and Mayor of Amsterdam, and son of a distinguished Professor of Law at Leiden. Patijn was one of a number of colleagues who came to stay with me in Scotland, where we conducted a number of hugely successful public meetings on European matters. And let it be said that Gwyneth Dunwoody, anti-Common Market MP, spoke Dutch and made great friends of Dutch MEPs such as Wilhelm Albers from Groenigen and Laisie Laben. Equally "anti-Europe", John Prescott was an enormous blunt and jovial success with European colleagues, and with the German Commissioner and former trade unionist Willy Haferkamp.

Above all the Europeans were pleased that the British Labour Delegation was led by the charming and effective former Foreign Secretary Michael Stewart, an orator of eloquence, exuding his First Class honours in Greats. He nominated the accountant Donald, Lord Bruce of Donnington, Aneurin Bevan's PPS in the 1945 Government, and me as members of the Budget Committee. It helped greatly that we got on famously with the current Chairman, Erwin Lange, a Socialist who opposed Nazis and who had been sent to the Eastern front as a member of the Punishment Brigade. The meetings were serious, particularly when heavyweights such as the German Economics Minister Graf Lamsdorff came for 2 ½ hour sessions. Within weeks I tumbled to it that our German colleagues were superbly briefed by the Bundesbank. So I asked Harold Wilson if I could be briefed by the Bank of England. Immediately he arranged this, by a senior official, Kit McMahon (later Sir, and Chairman of the Midland Bank and of much else). Crucially the staff of the Budget Committee were exceedingly able. Headed by the Sicilian Sergio Guccione, with M. Giraud, clever product of the Ecole Normale Superieure as his deputy, two then junior members, Julian Priestley (later to become Secretary General of the European Parliament) and the Irishman Eoghan O'Hannrahan both of whom I count as life-long friends, shepherded us through the ways of Community financial structure.

Then there were the members of the European Commission. Claude Cheysson, the Budget Commissioner and later Foreign Minister of France, asked Bruce and myself to dine at his favourite small restaurant in Strasbourg; we formed a personal working relationship. The British Commissioners, Christopher Soames and George Morgan Thomson, went out of their way to be helpful. Perhaps the President of the Commission Francois Xavier Ortoli entertained some of the doubts of General de Gaulle, but the friendly attitude of Guido Brunner, the other German Commissioner, and the impressive Dane, Finn Olav Gundelach, was shown by both being willing guests of my wife and myself in Scotland. On a memorable occasion in 1977, Gundelach addressed the Joint Shop Stewards' Committee of British Leyland, Bathgate – then employing 7500 people - and won them to the European cause, to my delight and relief. I never had my constituency make problems about my being an ardent European, partly be-cause every night from Brussels, Luxembourg or Strasbourg I would telephone a snippet about the Parliament to local Radio Forth. What really stirred my constituents were my efforts in the Parliament on behalf of the Scottish Pigeon Fanciers over problems of shooting, and Newcastle's disease (pigeon slimy shit!)

On my second week in Strasbourg I was the source of much ribald mer-riment. Rather than the Holiday Inn or Sofitel, I stayed in a small *pension* up the canal. In my blue track suit, I went for early morning runs in the Or-angerie. Unbeknown to me, but also in blue track suits, so did trainees from the French Foreign Legion. To the hilarious amusement of Bob Mitchell, MP for Southampton, and Mark Hughes, MP for Durham, out for an early morning stroll, I was apprehended by the French NCO in charge of recruits. I was subject to invective even more picturesque than I had received 25 years before from the drill sergeant of the Irish Guards (who was well remembered for having addressed the King of Jordan on the parade ground as "You dirty little King, Sir!").

Another occasion when I was the subject of restrained hilarity from Euro-pean colleagues was when Heinrich Aigner MEP for Regensburg/Passau, and then Chairman of the Budget Sub-Committee (equivalent to the UK's Public Accounts Committee), nominated Martin Bangemann, the Earl of Bessborough and myself to go to Friuli, to see if EEC funds had been misused in the after-math of the earthquake. I went to my friend, Ludwig Fellermaier, Chairman of the Socialist Group, and said, "We must have a couple of Italians with us." He shook his head, "They will not go; I have approached Altiero Spinelli." So I took it upon myself to approach the boss of the Italian Christian Democrats. Through an interpreter, I asked "Surely, you could send one of your colleagues with us to Friuli?" As she heard the reply, the interpreter gulped and blushed. "Well," I asked, "what did he say?" She gulped again, "He told you not to be a silly child, wet behind the ears." The boss was one of the most street-wise politicians in Europe, seven times Prime Minister of Italy, Giulio Andreotti.

There were many differences from the UK. It was a good time. And hemicir-cular politics are different from adversarial politics.

Michael Shaw

Towards a better financial regulation

As a member of the first delegation of M.P.s who were chosen to join the European Parliament, my lasting memory has always been of the great expense and inconvenience with which the new Parliament was burdened by its double existence in Brussels and Strasbourg.

So far as my own political activities in the European Parliament of those years are concerned, I remember, mainly, the good fortune that made me the rapporteur of two important pieces of legislation that affected the whole future of the Common Market.

The first relates to my being made the rapporteur of the 1978 Draft General Budget. This budget was created in anticipation of the impending European Direct Elections. This would mean that the voices and views of the people of all our member countries would be heard directly through their elected representatives. Thus, it was believed, they would, in the future, be heard in the budget processes of the Community. We recognised, in our deliberations, the responsibility of disciplining the creation of future Community resources needed to finance the Community policies that were being developed. Our various Committees studied and reported on the various proposals in the draft budget. In particular, we did our best to restrain the potential cost commitments that were being proposed for the enlargement of the Community. I can only say that we did our best.

My other recollection was of my appointment as rapporteur of a draft Financial Regulation. This had been put forward to us by Claude Cheysson, just before he retired as Commissioner. I had approached him and asked him to do this, because the existing Regulation was clearly quite inadequate. Happily, he kindly responded to my request and, as the draft went through the due processes in the European Parliament, I am equally happy to recall the helpful attitude that was taken to our work by Christopher Tugendhat, his successor. The resulting Financial Regulation was, in my view, a great credit to the hard work of my Finance Committee and, in particular, of the Parliamentary staff that helped us, especially Eoghan O'Hannrahan and Julian Priestley. My only comment is to recall that I believe the Community Accounts have never received a clear audit report since.

Julian Priestley
Thrown in at the deep end

At university in-between time misspent at the Union, with the Labour Club and the odd tutorial, I founded in 1971 the Oxford Committee for Europe with Sarah Rippon, daughter of Geoffrey, the Europe Minister leading accession negotiations. After graduation in 1972 I got a job in the European Movement organising youth support for entry. With some others including Tony Baldry, now a veteran Tory MP and Tom Spencer, later a long serving Tory MEP, and Andrew Neil, later editor of the Sunday Times, I organised at Cambridge at Easter 1973 a conference on European political parties with youth sections of several dozen national parties. We put on a mock European Parliament and asked one of the EP directors to give an introductory talk, explaining how the EP worked.

He rang me up several days after the event. I feared he was going to ask why he had received no expenses for his pains but in the event he invited me to come to Strasbourg for a job interview. Until then my future plans had been focussed on getting into the UK parliament as quickly as possible. But you don't get a salary as a prospective parliamentary candidate: and with my job with the European Movement coming to an end, I accepted his invitation.

The interview took place in Strasbourg in late April. I was totally unqualified for any administrative position. But I had one advantage. My gap year had been spent as a trainee in the Société Générale where no linguistic quarter was given and I could speak French fairly fluently. This was not the case of any of the other candidates called for interview. This was unfortunate as all the proceedings were indeed in French. So at the age of 22 I got the job as a temporary administrator in the EP committee service.

I pitched up in Luxembourg in the middle of June, was placed in the corner of someone else's office, waiting to be assigned to a committee. A day later I was told that I would be in the secretariat of the Budgets Committee, and instructed to read the Treaty, the Financial Regulations and some recent reports. The secretariat returned from a Brussels meeting of the committee on the third day. The head of the secretariat, a Sicilian who spoke French at breakneck speed gave me a ninety minute introduction into the very special world of EC budgetary questions, and informed me that I would immediately be assigned to be the main assistant to the general rapporteur for the 1974 Budget, an Ulster Unionist called Rafton Pounder. As he spoke not a word of French I was his only contact with anyone in the immediate working environment.

At the end of the week the team headed off to Brussels for another meeting. The chair of the committee, a French socialist called Georges Spénale, mayor of St Sulpice and part-time poet gave an hour-long introduction to his proposals to reform the EU budgetary procedure, and which ultimately became the 1975 Treaty on budgetary powers. It was a *tour de force*. And I was hooked. From what was a job to fill in the months before the good voters of Plymouth would do their duty and vote me in as their Labour MP, I found myself drawn into this very particular world. Even then the idea that this obscure part-time international assembly was fighting for and winning powers, that it would come to hold the Commission to account and, under certain circumstances, even overrule the Council: all this to a naïve idealistic political activist seemed the stuff of dreams.

The work on the 1974 budget was hard grind: the hundreds of amendments, the line-by-line *collationments* of the report with translators (very scornful about the writing skills of a relative of J B Priestley), everything typed up on baryts, corrected with tipex, and stapled together into reports by the production staff in a windowless room in the basement of the new Robert Schumann building at the Plateau de Kirchberg. Pounder and his young sidekick took quite some flak, not least from the committee chair, but we got through it, using the new post-1970 procedure, but not yet the greater powers which would be conferred on the EP in 1975.

I did three more general budgets (with Lord Bruce of Donington, an old Labour warhorse who had been a junior minister in the 1945 government, with

Michael Shaw, a gentle Tory moderate from Scarborough; and with Piet Dankert for the 1980 budget). It was in December 1979, just after direct elections, that the EP rejected the whole EC budget. I had the privilege of drafting the notorious rejection motion late at night on the kitchen table in a colleague's flat in Brussels. This seemed to me high politics.

And over time, with the hostility to Labour pro-Europeans and the massive defeat I suffered at my third attempt to get into the House of Commons against David Owen and Ann Widdecombe in 1983, my thirst for a UK parliamentary career waned.

In 1973 I had come to Luxembourg as a tyro administrator for what I thought would be a few months. I stayed in the service of the EP for the whole of my working life. And I never regretted it.

David Harley

Quiet days in Luxembourg

How strange it felt to have ended up in such a small and quiet country (or so it seemed from my office in the tower building, overlooking the edge of the forest, on the Plateau de Kirchberg outside the grey and windy city of Luxembourg) yet somehow being swept up to play a part, however modest, in such a grand adventure on a continental scale!

This contrast and dissonance between the slow and heavy rhythm of the internal bureaucratic routine and the scope and pace of external events and decisions was to remain a feature of my life in the European Parliament, in Luxembourg, Strasbourg and Brussels, for the next thirty-five years.

The British were warmly welcomed in those first years. "At last!", people would say, "What took you so long?" As though UK membership, although delayed, was a natural evolution which would give the Community a new and healthy balance, more rounded. It was believed that the arrival of the Brits, together with the Irish and the Danes, would give the European project a fresh dimension, would make it more grounded in practical and pragmatic advantage (rather than just in integration for integration's sake), would even make it more forward-looking.

It was a time of coming together in the interests of the cause, and of much hope and expectation.

Much was made too about the UK's unique parliamentary tradition: here surely, it was felt, Britain would make a decisive and much-needed contribution to the Community's development.

And so it proved, in the nominated Parliament during the initial period after UK accession, with the firm leadership of the British Conservatives by the much-respected Sir Peter Kirk and the barely less interesting contribution eventually made by the first two leaders of the Labour MEPs, Michael Stewart and John Prescott.

In 1975 came the UK referendum and the resounding two-thirds majority for the "Yes" camp.

Shortly afterwards Harold Wilson resigned "to make way for an older man" - Jim Callaghan, whose Labour Government duly approved the decision to elect the European Parliament by direct universal suffrage.

There was some disbelief and apprehension in the upper echelons of the European Parliament secretariat, admitted only privately or over lunch in the Grand-Duchy golf club, regarding the institution's capacity to effectively serve and administer the world's first-ever directly elected multinational parliament. But it turned out to be only stage fright, probably just as well in order to concentrate minds, and the newly constituted "Assembly" quickly confounded the doubters.

They were warm, heady and unforgettable nights during that first constituent session in July 1979. It seemed that Europe's entire political class had gathered to bear witness to this indispensable stage in the post-war continent's long and arduous journey to secure lasting peace and prosperity for the generations to come.

The most memorable evening of all was the day of the election of Simone Veil as the directly elected Parliament's first President. The symbolism was powerful, immediate and beyond words.

Those of us who were there that night and during those early years were immeasurably fortunate and privileged.

The pressmen

Robert Jarrett

The precursor

I became a European official in 1966, seven years before I became a European citizen. From the start the institutions employed a small number of Brits in the press and information field.

Before that, from 1961 to 1966, I was "executive secretary" of the Common Market Campaign and then of Britain in Europe, also of the Labour Common Market Committee (which in 1963 became the Labour Committee for Europe), and responsible for Europe House, the Young European Left, the Young European Management Association, and the Committee of Student European Associations. This grand complex of high-minded organisations occupied a small and under-equipped office where my functions ranged from that of chief executive to tea maker and stamp licker, aided by one gallant typist and a varying team of volunteer Europhiles. In 1965, Roy Pryce, then head of the information section of the Commission's London office (at that time officially the ECSC Delegation) rang me. He was returning to academe, and his deputy was also leaving, to work for Conservative Central Office. Derek Prag was returning from Luxembourg to take over Roy's job. The political affiliations would thus be reversed. To keep the balance they therefore needed a "socialist" for the second post! I started in February 1966.

Initially it was just Derek and me, ably supported by Valerie Williams in the library - and secretaries equipped with ultra-modern electric typewriters! As head of the office Derek oversaw generally, and dealt specifically with the press and the Tories. My title was Information Officer and I was expected to answer questions from, write articles for, give talks to organisations ranging from Labour Party and trade union groups, trade and employers' associations, NFU branches, university associations, and anyone else who asked. Luckily for me, the "Common Market" of then was far less complex than the EU of now, and the level of public knowledge on matters European was anyway not very high. So it was not too difficult to keep one jump ahead. But the pressure was increasing and after a while reinforcements were needed; Roger Broad also came back from Luxembourg to be Press Officer; and a bit later, to my great relief, Michael Berendt joined us to take responsibility for information on the CAP.

During this time I visited Brussels and sometimes Luxembourg every couple of months or so, for briefings and meetings, but often accompanying groups making an information visit to the institutions: MPs, journalists, trade union leaders.

The Berlaymont, opened in 1967 and intended to house most of the Commission staff of around 3,000, was very different from today. Most of the staff saw themselves as pioneers building Europe rather than civil servants administering it. The atmosphere was very informal, and there was minimal security - you just walked in! In 1967 Jean Rey followed Walter Hallstein as Commission President. Hallstein I never met, but Rey's door was always open. He invited me to drop by whenever I was in town to brief him on UK attitudes. He was not always free, but if he was, we would talk for maybe 15 or 20 minutes. Imagine an A5 just dropping in to see the President, without an appointment. Unthinkable since long ago! But then, apart from linguists and a few scientific staff, we were only half a dozen Brits on the pay roll.

I moved to Brussels in 1973 and worked with George Thomson, partly on regional policy, and partly attached to his *cabinet* during the run-up to the 1975 referendum, before moving on to other jobs as Head of Audiovisual and finally in External Relations. But from 1973 on I was just one of the growing crowd. Brits in Brussels were no longer special, though we were welcomed with enthusiasm. It took a little time before the others began to feel they had invited a cuckoo into their nest.

Michael Berendt

« Plus ça change …»

Who'd have thought that the themes which haunted us as we settled into the elegant splendour of Number 20 Kensington Palace Gardens in 1973 would still confront us in 2013: agriculture, fisheries, the EEC budget, myths and legends and, of course, British membership of the EEC. These were our staple diet as we came together under head of office Richard Mayne to form an enlarged European Commission UK information office, moving from previous premises in Chesham Street, to be joined by the European Parliament office under Roger Broad.

We were a mixed bunch. Anthony Hartley our right wing intellectual, one time editor of the Penguin book of French verse and credited with the phrase Angry Young Men to describe the Osborne/Amis/Larkin coterie; Michael Lake from the Guardian, battlefront correspondent in the Iceland Cod Wars and sometime of the Sun (pre-Murdoch of course); Michael Lloyd from the TUC and Robert Sheaf, aficionado of the theatre. I was landed with agriculture. A formidable group of secretarial staff – one-to-one in those days – had to deal with this motley crew.

Number 20 Kensington Palace Gardens was a grand address, which is today occupied by the Sultan of Brunei. We had, among others, the Soviet embassy to the right and across the tree-lined avenue, the Lebanese to the left, Egypt in the middle, Israel at the bottom of the road and uniformed watchmen at each end, so we were in select company. The house at the top had been MI19's Cage where Nazi prisoners were interrogated during and after the war.

Our mansion was where many candidates for posts in Brussels were interviewed during that first year. I had made the mistake of putting some knowledge of Danish on the application form and theatre as one of my interests, but was somewhat challenged when a Danish member of the jury threw me a theatre question in his own language. Had it been about pigs I could have coped. Luckily Tony Morris was also on the jury.

The Information Office was frequently on the defensive as Europe remained the enduring fault line in British politics, but at that time it was the Labour Party which was deeply split. The party refused to nominate members for the UK delegation to the European Parliament, most trade unions boycotted the European TUC, and a resolution to quit the EEC without any negotiation whatever was only narrowly defeated at the October Labour Party conference.

Some of the key chapters of the enlargement negotiations were unresolved at the time of British entry, including the terms for Commonwealth sugar imports, access for New Zealand milk products and the basis for Britain's EEC budget contributions, so there was still doubt over Britain's long-term future in Europe. The export of 200,000 tonnes of EEC butter to Russia at 8p a pound caused outcry, although a scheme was launched to subsidise butter sales to Britain's poor in an effort to calm public indignation. World agricultural prices had risen, but farm surpluses still weighed heavily on public perception – and on the budget. The Keep Britain Out organisation changed its name to Get Britain Out.

The situation was not helped by a raft of troubles affecting Edward Heath's Conservative government – a European currency crisis triggering a steep fall in the pound, bitter divisions in Ulster, the threat of a second miners' strike and – in October – the Yom Kippur war followed by an Arab boycott of oil supplies and an unseemly scramble between the member states to do their own deals. Not much solidarity there.

Brussels seemed rather remote. Communication was by telex, the typewriter was king. It was Hartley who recommended offering lunch to Commission colleagues on our occasional visits to the Berlaymont – he was a firm believer in thus building personal relationships. We organised visits for press and political groups, each of which left memories. One industrial correspondent spent a night in the Gran' Place jail.

What we could not know in 1973 was that Heath would call a general election early the following year under the pressure of a second miners' strike, that Harold Wilson would become prime minister and that he would commit the UK to a referendum to settle the question of membership for good and all – once the terms had been "renegotiated". So how, I wonder, will history repeat itself 40 years on?

Michael Lake
The 1975 referendum

My wife and I, newly married, sailed from Auckland for England on the SS Arcadia and arrived in London in February, 1961. Three months later I found myself economics correspondent in the Fleet Street office of The Scotsman, one month before Harold Macmillan announced that the Government would ask if the UK could join the Common Market. I had to go to the Treasury to be briefed on what it was. I subsequently covered every step of the doomed Heath negotiations, from the opening on October 13, 1961, to the veto on January 29, 1963 and Heath's final off the record press conference in the Hotel Metropole in Brussels to 300 national and foreign journalists. (Uniquely, and it was never published, he got a standing ovation.)

For 12 years I covered the Brussels beat for The Scotsman, the old Daily Herald and its successor, the pre-Murdoch Sun, as its diplomatic correspondent.

In January 1973 I had been on The Guardian for three years. One day I telephoned old friend Roger Broad, then the Commission's press officer in London, to ask him something or other. I knew he was about to become the Head of the London office of the European Parliament so I asked him, quite interested to know, who was going to do his job at the Commission. He said: "Why don't you do it? I can fix it with Gwyn Morgan." It was time to see things from the inside. It was as simple as that. I don't recall any paperwork. I briefly appeared before a board, three members of which I knew, and had a medical. It turned out I was one of 450-odd Brits being fast-tracked into the Brussels institutions.

I started work in the London Office of the Commission on October 1, 1973, sharing a first floor office at 20 Kensington Palace Gardens with two other people, all assigned to cutting and pasting press clippings. In a moment of despair I wondered if this was why I had left my senior job at The Guardian. Could I go back? On the third day I ascended to the third floor and occupied the vacated bedroom of the Commission's former head of delegation, Georges Berthoin, for the next four years.

Then came the 1975 referendum. This was better than the three-day week, blackouts and candles. I found myself rather in clover: not only did I know the story well having covered it for 12 years, most of the journalists were old mates.

Among the statistics of this period I recall that the London Office spent two thirds of DG-X's entire visits budget in 1974-75 and that I spent two thirds of that, accompanying dozens of journalists on twice-monthly trips to Brussels. For once these trips were not just for jaded specialist "European" reporters: I invited all sorts of other specialised writers plus the "back bench" people: editors, women's editors, columnists, foreign editors, production and night editors, sub-editors, political staff, leader writers - those who wrote unfettered or decided what, and how much, would be printed or broadcast. I staged conferences in the regions for local journalists. I believe I visited all the dailies in the country. And of course I took my share of baby-minding visiting Commissioners.

The Commission's London Office was almost, but not quite, drowning in calls. The Foreign Office set up a special help line for the public, then, bereft, asked us to deflect callers there. We did, but we remained flooded. Meanwhile dozens of journalists from the sticks called for expertise to help them write stories with a local impact. The trick was, of course, to clarify the officialese. While one day indicating (actually dictating) an editorial to a hapless leader writer on deadline from somewhere up north I inadvertently reverted to old habits and dictated: "Stop, para." The leader-writer didn't notice, just typed on. Much of Jon Lander's acclaimed six-part series on the referendum for ITN was prepared during his many visits to my office. The News of the World called to confirm correctly that Article 48 of the Treaty of Rome outlawed any attempt to ban the famous Johan Cruyff, a Common Market worker, from playing for an English football club. That story probably won a million votes. Or not.

It was a truly hectic, relentless and exhilarating period. The last newspaper to fall in line and advocate YES was the Dundee Courier, no doubt after it examined the terms of entry relating to jute. On victory day we London staff inadvertently bought ourselves two orders of champagne, and drank the lot.

Martin Vasey

The spokesman

In November 1971 I moved from Strasbourg, where I had worked for the Council of Europe, to Brussels so as to be present at the birth of the enlarged Community as a free-lance journalist. In January 1973 I took a full time job with The Economist which had belatedly decided to open a Brussels office. As I had followed the EEC in one job or another for the previous ten years I had no learning curve to go through. This was not true for many of my new London-based colleagues who beat a path to our door to be briefed on this strange creature called the Common Market. Not only journalists either. I was given an excellent lunch by a City banker who plied me with questions about the inner workings of the Commission and the Council. I apologised for my near total ignorance of the banking sector, but he assured me that what I had given him was much more valuable since "No-one in London has any idea how the place works". To make matters worse, Whitehall tended to regard as confidential documents freely available in Brussels.

Sometime in the spring I heard that there was an opening for a British journalist to be the press spokesman for Sir Christopher Soames, the senior British member of the Commission. I immediately went to see the chief spokesman, Bino Olivi, and his deputy, Manuel Santarelli. They were delighted to recruit a member of the Brussels press corps rather than have an unknown quantity from London. I was vetted by Sir Christopher's *chef de cabinet* David Hannay whom I already knew; sailed through the formal interview which was conducted exclusively in French; and duly arrived at the Berlaymont on 1 September. Typically, my application form had got lost and no one was expecting me, but it didn't seem to matter.

The Spokesman's Group, as the Commission's press service was then called, was a hybrid service. The Spokesman himself, who was responsible directly to the President, attended the weekly meetings of the Commission on Wednesday and informed the press of the outcome the following day at the daily press briefing (the biggest daily gathering of journalists anywhere in Europe). The rest of the week briefings were usually left to the members of the Group, who each covered the sector of responsibility of a different member of the Commission (in those days invariably of the same nationality). We therefore served two masters: the Commission as a body; and our individual Commissioners with their own political priorities. We still operated very much as a group. Our offices were next door to the press room, we briefed each other every morning, and we all mixed with the press at the briefing. The press corps was then dominated by journalists from the founder member states who had been there since the beginning and were all convinced Europeans. At formal press conferences by members of the Commission interpretation was provided; otherwise all the proceedings were in French, a practice which lasted for another 20 years.

Bino Olivi was one of the first generation of Commission officials who had served under the legendary Hallstein. As Spokesman, he regaled our morning meetings with caustic accounts of the debates in the Commission but otherwise left us a more or less free hand. On the other hand, David Hannay, as Soames' *chef de cabinet*, ran a very tight ship; I was never left in any doubt as to what I was to say (and not to say) in the external relations field.

As Vice-President responsible for this area, Soames was in his element. Not a man to concern himself overmuch with policy detail, he was superb at dealing with visiting US congressmen, Commonwealth prime ministers or Middle Eastern and Asian dignitaries, who arrived unsure how to react to this new great power in world trade. He was also impressive with foreign journalists. I once organised an interview with the great man for a German journalist at the time of Harold Wilson's "renegotiation", which we all had difficulties in explaining. The journalist began with a diatribe against the British government in the form of a 12-line question read out at high speed. Soames leaned back in his chair with a broad smile. "All my life," he began, "I have believed - passionately - in Europe". He then took off for the stratosphere where he remained for the rest of the interview, completely ignoring any questions he did not like. The journalist was delighted, though he subsequently told me that they had had difficulty in translating the interview into German since Soames broad brush approach did not always involve the use of verbs. But what a performance!

Epilogue

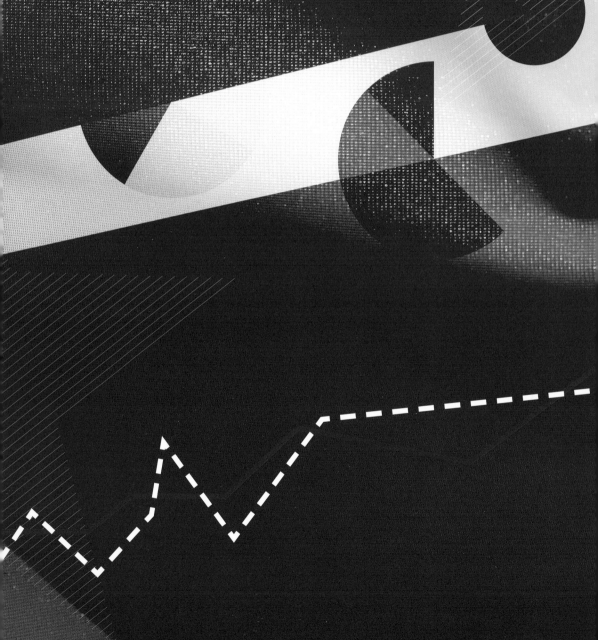

The overall picture

It is useful to look at the personal contributions to this book in the wider context of UK recruitment to the European institutions immediately after accession. Surprisingly little analysis of UK recruitment to the European institutions following accession has been done. However, in her book *Britons in Brussels: Officials in the European Commission and Council Secretariat*[7], Virginia Willis looked at this question. Through interviews with individuals, and based on contributions from Whitehall, the Commission and the Council, she analysed the backgrounds of those who went to Brussels initially, described their experience and related it to Whitehall perspectives and procedures. She also carried out herself a limited survey of a random sample of 15% of British staff.

By 31 December 1974 there were 296 UK A grade staff appointed, 14.9% of the total Commission A grade staff, 100 B grade (7.3%), 87 C grade (3.3%), 6D (1.7%) and 106 LA (13.6%) making a total of 595 British staff or 8.4% of the total Commission staff. These proportions were below those of France, Germany and Italy. Over the next five years 60 UK staff resigned out of a total of 226 staff for the Commission as a whole. 26 British departures were at A grade out of 35 total A grade departures in that period.

Willis concluded that the special recruitment exercise of 1972-1973 was crucial in determining the future shape and quality of UK staffing of the community institutions. She found that only very informal records had been kept of professional backgrounds of the new recruits. In general terms the majority of the British officials came from the wider public sector. One third came from the Civil Service and FCO (50% at A1 and A2 level), 10% from overseas and international civil servants (i.e. UN, OECD, Council of Europe and Commonwealth Secretariat), and a number were former colonial officials who went into DG VIII. A number of recruits came from the nationalised industries and also some from local government. There was a comparatively large contingent from academic or semi-academic bodies. Recruitment from the private sector was about 40%. Willis suggests that this may have reflected the then unfavourable economic climate in the UK. This recruitment was concentrated in middle and junior grades. A sizeable contingent came from the professions at A4-A5. Few trade unionists were appointed.

---

7   Virginia Willis *Britons in Brussels : officials in the European Commission and Council Secretariat* London 1980, published jointly
     by the European Centre for Political Studies and the Royal Institute of Public Administration (ISBN 0853742170)

Willis compared this with a 1972 Commission paper showing the backgrounds of A grades before enlargement: 50% coming from national administrations, 23% from the private sector and 28% from professional associations and trade unions. The Commission study had also analysed the educational background of 1000 officials which showed 28% had law degrees, 14% economics degrees 10% were political scientists. 30% had other degrees, 18% had either not completed their degrees or did not have one.

The survey carried out by Willis of the backgrounds of the UK recruits showed that many had an economics bias, followed by language graduates, and then by graduates in law, history, politics and European studies. Only two had scientific degrees and three were agricultural specialists. 60% of the UK contingent had postgraduate degrees and almost half had first degrees from Oxford and Cambridge universities, with graduates of the LSE and the Scottish universities the next most numerous.

Comparatively few Britons arrived in Brussels who had not already had experience of living, working or studying abroad, or a family connection with Europe, or contact with the Community institutions. 60% of the survey group owned to long-existing pro-European Community feelings, although very few had been active in promoting UK membership. 57% admitted that dissatisfaction with their previous jobs or career prospects played a major role in a decision to make a radical change in their lives. 50% said scales of remuneration were an attraction but only 6% knew what net income to expect on their arrival in Brussels (34% were amazed to find how much more they earned than they had expected).

A high proportion of spouses of the survey group had previous experience of living outside the UK. 10% of those appointed were bachelors and 20% were divorced or separated at or soon after their arrival. In general apart from the civil servants who had return tickets very few had a firm possibility of return if the venture was not a success. They had a pragmatic intention to see what it was like and how they got on.

Willis concluded that a picture emerged of Britons arriving in Brussels in 1973-1974 in an unfamiliar, challenging and often difficult environment, where the potential for frustration was greater than usually encountered but where the real and psychological rewards were high enough to outweigh this frustration. The recruits found jobs varied enormously in their scope and value but that an able, enterprising and adaptable person could build a career that became exceptional in its importance, influence and satisfaction. Where working methods were alien the influence of Britain and the other new member states had succeeded in adapting them a little.

Any difficulties arose chiefly from the distinctive and multinational character of the organisation. Many Britons at an individual level were slow to realise the degree to which job and promotion prospects depended on their own efforts at managing their careers. At the same time, compared to what they felt was the case for their colleagues of other nationalities, they felt insufficiently supported in those efforts by UKRep or (for those in the Commission) the UK Commissioners' *cabinets*.

Appendices

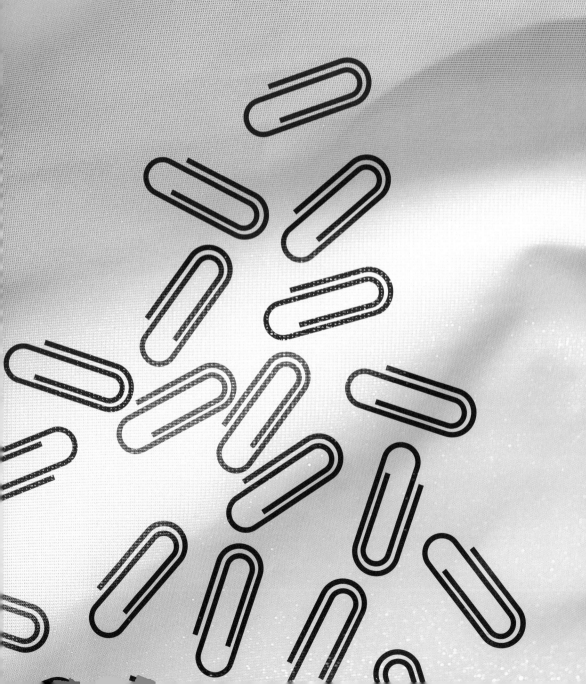

List of Contributors with brief biographical details

Liliana Archibald worked as a broker at Lloyds specialising in export credits before being appointed head of the export credits division in DGI (external relations) in March 1973. She left the Commission in 1977 to return to London but remained involved in European affairs.

Nicholas Argyris was an economic adviser in the Board of Trade before going to work in the state aids division of DGIV (competition) in November 1973. He later worked in DG VIII (development), DGXVII (Energy), and DGXIII (Information society), ending as director of Telecommunications.

Keith Arrowsmith was working for the Royal Institution of Chartered Surveyors before joining DGVI (agriculture) where he took responsibility for food aid.

Paul Atkins was a free-lance translator in London with experience in the steel industry. He joined the ECSC translation service in Luxembourg in June 1973.

Sir Christopher Audland joined the Foreign Office in 1948, and was involved in the first British bid for membership of the European Communities. He was Deputy Secretary General of the Commission from March 1973 to 1981, and then Director General for Energy (DGXVII) 1981 – 1986.

Graham Avery began his career in the Ministry of Agriculture, Fisheries and Food (MAFF), where he worked on UK entry to the EEC. He was a member of Sir Christopher Soames' *cabinet* 1973 - 76. He later advised Roy Jenkins, President of the Commission 1977-81, as well as successive Commissioners for agriculture. He held senior posts in DGVI (agriculture) and DGI (external relations) as well as the Task Force for Enlargement.

Jo Bell trained as a nurse at Bristol Royal Hospital. She lived in Ispra, where her husband worked at the Joint Research Centre establishment. Following his death, she joined the Commission's medical service in Brussels in May 1973, where she stayed until retirement.

Michael Berendt was an agricultural journalist before joining the Commission's London office in 1971, first as the farming specialist, then as press officer. In 1981 he moved to Brussels as a member of the *cabinet* of Ivor Richards and subsequently as spokesman for Clinton Davis and Sir Leon Brittan. He left in 1991 to become a consultant on European affairs.

Martyn Bond was a university lecturer in West European Studies in Northern Ireland. In 1974 he joined the Council of Minister's General Secretariat where he stayed until 1988 (apart from two years as BBC correspondent in Berlin 1981 – 83). He was Head of the Office of the European Parliament in the UK 1989-1999. He then worked for the Federal Trust.

Roger Broad was a journalist before going to work for the Commission on the press side in 1964, first in Luxembourg and then in London. In 1973 he was appointed first head of the London Office of the European Parliament.

Hugh Burton had 17 years' experience in company management in the UK, France and Spain when he joined the secretariat of the Economic and Social Committee at the beginning of 1974. He retired 23 years later as director of the joint services of the ESC and the Committee of the Regions.

Helen Campbell worked in Germany as a translator and DJ before moving to Brussels in 1971. In February 1973 she was recruited by the Commission as one of the first British trainee interpreters. Since retirement she has been involved in training student interpreters.

Anthony Caston was a specialist in recruitment with 20 years' experience in the private and university sectors when he joined DGIX (personnel and administration) in November 1973. He dealt successively with recruitment, pensions, the JSIS and the renewal of the staff regulations.

Hywel Ceri Jones worked in administration at the University of Sussex. In 1973 he was appointed as head of division for education and youth in DGXIII (education and research). He later became a director and acting, then deputy director general until he retired in 1998.

Margaret Cooper (formerly Young) had just finished a bilingual secretarial course when she joined the Commission in early 1973. She worked first in DGVIII (development) and then in the secretariat of Sir Christopher Audland before leaving in 1977 to get married.

Tam Dalyell, a teacher by background, was Labour MP for West Lothian 1962 – 83, Linlithgow 1983 – 2005, serving on many committees. He served as member of the unelected European Parliament 1975-79.

Robert Elphick spent most of his working life as a journalist working first for Reuters (Moscow, London, Algiers) and then the BBC (Vienna, Bonn, Vietnam, Beirut, India and Europe generally). He joined the Commission in 1977 as spokesman for Guido Brunner (energy) and subsequently for Christopher Tugendhat (budget). He ended his career in the Commission's London Office.

Sir Leslie Fielding served in the UK Diplomatic Service including posts in Teheran, Singapore, Phnom Penh and Paris. He joined the Commission as a director in DGI (external relations) in April 1973. He was subsequently head of the Commission's delegation in Tokyo before succeeding Sir Roy Denman as director general. He returned to the UK in 1987 to take up a university post.

Vivien Flynn joined the Commission translation services in Luxembourg in June 1973. She worked in the service for 30 years and left Luxembourg after 3 more years.

Sir Michael Franklin started his career in the Ministry of Agriculture, Fisheries and Food (MAFF) and was part of the British team during the accession negotiations. From 1973 to 1976 he was deputy director general of DGVI (agriculture), after which he returned to the UK Civil Service in the Cabinet Office and as Permanent Secretary in MAFF and the Board of Trade.

David Hannay (Lord Hannay of Chiswick) served in the Foreign Office in Tehran and Kabul, followed by seven years in the UK delegation to the European Communities in Brussels where he was involved in the accession negotiations. From 1973 to 1976 he was *chef de cabinet* to Sir Christopher Soames. Returning to the UK Diplomatic Service he was UK Permanent Representative to the EU 1985-90 and British Permanent Representative to the UN 1990-95. He is active in the House of Lords.

Michael Hardy worked for the UN legal service in New York before joining the Legal Service of the Commission in 1973. He moved to DGI (external relations) in 1978, and served as Head of the EC Delegation to the UN in New York from 1982-87. He was then director in DGXIII (Information technologies and telecommunications).

David Harley joined the secretariat of the European Parliament in 1975 and retired 35 years later. He was successively spokesman for the President, Director of Press and Media and Secretary General of the Socialist Group before becoming Deputy Secretary General of the Parliament.

Richard Hay joined the Treasury in 1963. 1973 – 82: *cabinet*s of Sir Christopher Soames (external relations) and Christopher Tughendhat (financial institutions, budget, financial control and personnel and administration); 1980 – 82 director, DGII (economic and financial affairs); 1982 – 91 DGIX (personnel and administration) first as deputy, then as director general. International President of AIACE 2011-14.

David Heath was an economist/statistician with French and German and experience of both the public and private sectors. He joined the Statistical Office in Luxembourg in May 1974.

George Helcké joined the Joint Research Centre at Ispra (Italy) in 1963, having been recruited by Euratom in 1962 when it was expected the UK would shortly be joining the EC.

Lorna Hoe joined the Commission as a secretary in April 1972. She later worked for the Danish Commissioner Finn Olaf Gundelach and continued working for successive Danish Commissioners until 1995.

Robert Hull left the North of England Development Council to become one of the youngest UK A7 officials in the Commission. From the Customs Union Service he moved to DGI (external relations). Later he was Assistant in DG XV (Financial Institutions and Company Law), head of Environment Policy Coordination in DGXI, and director in the Economic and Social Committee.

Sir Francis Jacobs taught at Glasgow University and LSE before moving to the Council of Europe in Strasbourg where he dealt with cases before the European Commission of Human Rights 1969-72. He was a legal secretary (*référendaire*) at the European Court of Justice in Luxembourg 1972-74, Professor of European Law at King's College, London and subsequently Advocate General at the ECJ 1988-2006.

Robert Jarrett after working for pro-European campaign organisations joined the information section of the Commission's London Office in 1966. He moved to Brussels in 1973, working first in DGXVI (regional policy), then as head of Audio-visual in DGX (Information) and finally in DGI (external relations).

Sir Michael Jenkins joined the Foreign Office in 1959 and served in Paris, Moscow and Bonn. From 1973 to 1976 he was first deputy and then *chef de cabinet* to George Thomson, and in 1977 adviser to Roy Jenkins. He then rejoined the Diplomatic Service, but returned to the Commission 1979 – 83 as head of the Central Advisory Group, and Deputy Secretary General. Later he served in the Diplomatic Service in Washington and as Ambassador to the Netherlands. He died on 31 March 2013.

Stanley Johnson worked for the World Bank, the Conservative Research Department and as a consultant for various UN specialised agencies. He was appointed head of division in the Commission's new environment and consumer protection service in April 1973. He was Conservative MEP for Wight and Hants East 1979 – 84; on returning to the Commission he was a special adviser in the new Directorate General for the environment 1984-90.

Michael Lake covered European affairs for various national newspapers before becoming the press officer for the Commission's London office 1973-1977. He was subsequently head of press and information first in New York and then Tokyo and served as head of the EU delegation in Ankara and Budapest.

Pamela Levy was already working in Brussels when she was recruited as a secretary in the Commission in May 1973, working in DGII and DGVIII.

Pamela Mayorcas joined the FCO in 1970 as a translator, working in the unit responsible for translating existing EC legislation into English. In May 1973 she joined the English section of the Euratom Translation Service Centre in Brussels.

Sir William Nicoll started his career in the Board of Trade (serving in India 1955-59). He served in the UK Representation in Brussels 1972 – 75 and 1977 – 82. He was a director general in the General Secretariat of the Council of Ministers 1982 – 91.

Sir Julian Priestley was a young graduate working for the European Movement when he took a post in the European Parliament secretariat in 1973, in the committee service. He was later Director of Parliamentary Committees, Secretary General of the Socialist Group 1989 – 94, and head of the private office of the President 1994 – 97. He became Secretary General 1997 – 2007.

Roy Pryce started working for the ECSC in 1957 but resigned as head of the information section of the London Office in 1965 to resume his university career. He returned to the Commission to serve as director in DGX (Information) 1973 – 79, before returning to the University of Sussex.

Nigel Robson was an agricultural economist and lecturer before joining the Commission in November 1973 in DGVI, later becoming a head of division. He took early retirement in 1998 but continued to manage research projects for DGIII (research and education) on a part-time basis.

Bill Robinson joined the UK Civil Service (10 Downing St, Cabinet Office, Treasury). He served as head of division in DGII (economic and financial affairs) 1974 – 78, before returning to London to work in the public, private and academic sectors including a period as Adviser to the Chancellor of the Exchequer, Nigel Lawson

Jonathan Scheele had a background in the private sector (Unilever and British Leyland) when he joined DGIII (industry) in the Commission in March 1974, later moving to DGI (external relations). He was subsequently head of the Commission delegation in Romania, before his final post as head of the Commission Representation in London.

Michael Shaw (Lord Shaw of Northstead, Baron of Liversedge) was Conservative MP for Brighouse and Spenborough 1960 – 64, for Scarborough and Whitby 1966 – 74, for Scarborough 1974 – 92. He was a member of the UK delegation to the European Parliament 1974-79.

George Thomson (Lord Thomson of Monifieth) was Labour MP for Dundee East 1952 – 72. He held different ministerial posts (including that of Commonwealth Secretary and Minister for Europe). He was one of the first two British Commissioners (with Sir Christopher Soames) 1973-76, taking responsibility for regional policy. From 1977 he served in different posts including Chair of the Advertising Standards Authority and the Independent Broadcasting Authority. He died in 2008.

Martin Vasey worked as a journalist in Luxembourg and Brussels apart from four years at the Council of Europe in Strasbourg before joining the Commission in September 1973 as press spokesman for Sir Christopher Soames. He later worked for German and Danish Commissioners, before moving to the Secretariat General.

Richard Wainwright was a barrister and legal adviser to BP. He joined the Commission's Legal Service in 1973. After an interlude as adviser in the *cabinet* of Clinton Davies, he became director/head of team dealing first with the internal market and then with competition, retiring in 2005.

Dennys Watson was senior partner and deputy head of European operations for a firm of management consultants, having worked in Germany, Italy and Belgium. He joined DGXVI (regional policy) in the Commission in late 1973.

George Wedell was Professor of Adult Education in the University of Manchester before being appointed head of the employment policy division in DGV (social affairs). On his return to the UK in 1982 he went back to Manchester University where he founded the European Institute for the Media.

Richard Wells served in the Board of Trade before joining George Thomson's *cabinet* in February 1973, where he dealt principally with agriculture, fisheries and budgetary questions. In 1977, he returned to the Board of Trade, where he later worked on the European structural funds (including grants for Gibraltar).

Edward Whitehead was recruited as a scientific official by Euratom in 1964. He worked in a succession of research institutes in France and Italy before ending up as administrator of research programmes in Brussels.

Christopher Wilkinson worked for the Commonwealth Secretariat, the OECD and the World Bank before joining the Commission in 1973 as head of division in DGVI (regional policy). He later worked in DGIII (internal market and industrial affairs) and DGXIII (telecommunications, information industries and innovation) where he dealt with the information society.

Glossary

A1, A2, A3, A4/5, A6/7: Ranks in the Community institutions' grading system for staff with a university degree which applied in 1973 and for the next 30 years (major changes were made in 2004). A1 was the rank of a director general (or deputy director general), the most senior grade; A2 that of a director; A3 that of a head of division; A4/5 that of a principal administrator; and A6/7 that of administrator – this level was in principle the normal recruitment level for graduate staff. Similar levels existed in the B (executive), C (clerical) and D (supporting) grades.

ACP: Africa, Caribbean and Pacific Group of States – the acronym given to former French colonies and to developing countries of the Commonwealth with which the enlarged Community negotiated a fresh association agreement to replace the earlier Yaoundé Agreement (the Lomé Convention)

AETR DOCTRINE: The principle, established by a judgement of the European Court of Justice , that the European Union's external competence is not confined to the explicit provisions in the treaties for example on trade, but is also derived from the Community's capacity to adopt "internal rules", for example on road transport (the subject of the ECJ ruling which gave the doctrine its name). Even when not exercised the existence of such powers under the treaties *ipso facto* confers external competence on the Community.

AIACE: Association internationale des anciens de l'Union européenne (previously: des Communautés européennes) ; the French initials of the former title are still used because the direct acronym is unpronounceable; the official denomination in English is now "International Association of Former Officials of the European Union". AIACE has over 9,500 members – roughly half the total of all pensioners of the EU institutions

BERLAYMONT: The iconic building with a curved, glass front, situated at the end of the Rue de la Loi. It has housed the Commission since 1967 (with a period between 1991 and 2004 when the building was completely renovated, in part to strip out asbestos which had been extensively used when first built). At the time covered by this book, the Commissioners met and had their offices on the 13th floor with some *cabinet* staff, most of whom were however on the 12th floor. At this time, too, most DG's were housed in the same building

BoT: UK Board of Trade; subsequently Department of Trade and Industry (DTI).

Cabinet: The private office that supports the President and each member of the European Commission

CAP: Common agricultural policy

CECA: French acronym for European Coal & Steel Community (ECSC)

CFP: Common fisheries policy

Coreper: Committee of Permanent Representatives of the member states responsible for preparing meetings of the Council of Ministers (the French acronym is always used)

COUNCIL OF EUROPE: The first European organisation set up in 1949 bringing together the democratic countries of the continent after WW2. Based in Strasbourg, its main achievement is the European Convention on Human Rights. With the spread of democracy first to the Iberian peninsular and then to central and eastern Europe it now has 47 members. It is quite separate from the EU.

DG: Directorate-General, the name given to the different departments of the Commission (see box)

DTI: UK Department of Trade & Industry

EC: European Communities, namely the ECSC, the EEC and Euratom. In 1965 the executives of the three communities were merged together. The three communities were shortened to European Community; later, in 1993 the communities were merged and absorbed into the EU under the Maastricht Treaty (though Euratom still has a separate identity)

ECJ: European Court of Justice based in Luxembourg

ECSC: European Community for Steel and Coal, sometimes referred to by its French initials (CECA). Established by the Treaty of Paris in 1951. Based in Luxembourg

EEC: European Economic Community established by one of the Treaties of Rome in 1957. Based in Brussels; in 1973 popularly known as the Common Market

EFTA: European Free Trade Area founded in 1960 as an alternative to the EEC. UK, Denmark and Ireland left EFTA on accession to the EEC in 1973. Four States remain: Iceland, Norway, Liechtenstein and Switzerland

EIB: European Investment Bank, founded in 1958 under the Treaty of Rome for the Community's nonprofit long-term lending; it works closely with other EU policy bodies

EP: European Parliament, with administrative headquarters in Luxembourg. Though now it has some plenary and many committee meetings in Brussels, at the time of this book most meetings were in Strasbourg or in Luxembourg

ESC: Economic and Social Committee, established under the EEC Treaty of Rome of 1957 to bring together representatives of the employers, the trade unions and civil society to give advice and to increase involvement in the workings of the EEC

Enarque: A graduate of the *Ecole nationale d'administration (ENA)*, an elite school for future top French civil servants

Etienne Davignon (Viscount): Belgian statesman & European Commissioner 1977-1985, who helped develop EC industrial policy

EU: European Union created by the Treaty of Maastricht 1993

Euratom: The European Atomic Energy Community, established by a Treaty of Rome in 1957; scientific research work by the EC has been based on this treaty

FAO: Food and Agriculture Organisation, a specialised agency of the United Nations based in Rome

FCO: UK Foreign and Commonwealth Office

GATT: General Agreement on Tariffs and Trade, renamed 1995 World Trade Organisation

INA: Institut National Agronomique, one of the French Grandes Ecoles

INRA: Institut National de la Recherche Agronomique

LUXEMBOURG COMPROMISE: In the summer of 1965 President de Gaulle withdrew French ministers and officials from the Council in order to reverse the supranational development of the EC institutions (the "empty chair policy"). The crisis lasted until January 1966 when it was agreed at a meeting in Luxembourg that decisions would not be taken by qualified majority as laid down in the EEC Treaty on matters deemed by a member state to involve "very important national interests". Although it had no legal validity the Luxembourg Compromise shaped the Community's decision-making for nearly 20 years and only fell into disuse after the signing of the Single European Act which laid the basis for the single market.

JRC (CCR): Joint Research Council, the branch of the Euratom Treaty which handles scientific research both at some large dedicated centres (the chief of which is at Ispra, in northern Italy) and in some national scientific laboratories

LS: Legal Service (both the Commission and the Council Secretariat have one)

MAFF: UK Ministry of Agriculture, Fisheries and Food

OECD: The Organisation for Economic Co-operation and Development (OECD) is an in-ternational economic organisation of 34 countries founded in 1961 to stimulate economic progress and world trade. It was the successor of the post-war (1948) Organisation for European Economic Co-operation (OEEC)

RAPPORTEUR: The title given in the European Parliament (and used similarly elsewhere) to the member who takes the lead in analysing a proposal, collecting comments, and presenting a report to the relevant committee and then to the plenary session for decision

SME: Small and medium enterprises

STAGES: French word for training posts, thus stagiaires = trainees

UKDEL: United Kingdom Delegation to the European Communities, until accession when it became UKRep

UKREP: The United Kingdom Permanent Representation to the European Union in Brussels represents the UK in the workings of the EU, chiefly in preparing the work of the Council of Ministers. The UK Permanent Representative represents the UK on Coreper

WERNER PLAN (or REPORT): At the European Summit in The Hague in 1969, the Heads of State and Government agreed to prepare a plan for economic and monetary Union by 1980. It was drawn up by a working group chaired by Pierre Werner, Luxembourg's Minister for Finance(1953 - 59) and Prime Minister (1959 – 74; 1979 - 84), and presented in October 1970. It was never implemented

List of Commission Departments in 1973 (with changes by 1982)

	In 1973	In 1982, if changed
	Secretariat General	
	Legal Service	
	Spokesman's Group	
	Statistical Office	
I	External Relations	
II	Economic and Financial Affairs	
III	Industrial and Technological Affairs	Internal Market and Industrial Affairs
IV	Competition	
V	Social Affairs	Employment, Social Affairs and Education
VI	Agriculture	
VII	Transport	
VIII	Development and Cooperation	Development
IX	Personnel and Administration	
X	Information	
XI	Internal Market	Environment and Consumer Protection
XII	Research, Science and Education	Science, Research and Development
	Joint Research Centre	
XIII	Scientific and Technical Information	Information Market and Innovation
XIV		Fisheries
XV	Financial Institutions and Taxation	
XVI	Regional Policy	
XVII	Energy	
XVIII	Credits and Investments	
XIX	Budgets	
XX	Financial Control	
	Joint Service for Conference Interpretation	
	Security Office	
	Office for Official Publications of the European Communities	
	Euratom Supply Agency	

The names of DGs (especially DGs XII and XIII) have continued to evolve since the period covered, in line with changing policy objectives and responsibilities, and the addition of some new services. In 2004 the numbering of services was replaced by acronyms.